About the Author

Ellen Norman Stern was born in Germany. She grew up in Louisville, Kentucky, and was graduated from the University of Louisville.

Mrs. Stern worked at television station WAVE-TV for several years, then joined the production staff of a major national television network in New York.

She has written stories and articles ever since her junior high school days, many of them with a historical background. Her first book, *Embattled Justice* (the story of Louis D. Brandeis), was published in 1971.

Ellen Stern, her husband, and their two sons currently live in a suburb of Philadelphia.

DREAMER
IN THE
DESERT

A Profile of Nelson Glueck

DREAMER IN THE DESERT

A Profile of Nelson Glueck

by ELLEN NORMAN STERN

KTAV Publishing House, Inc. • New York

Library of Congress Cataloging in Publication Data

Stern, Ellen Norman.
  Dreamer in the desert.

  Bibliography: p.
  Includes index.
  1. Gleuck, Nelson, 1900-   2. Scholars, Jewish—
United States—Biography. I. Title.
BM775.G56S74   221.9′3 [B]   79-23707
ISBN 0-87068-656-9

BM
755
.G56
S74

Manufactured in the United States of America

For
RABBI RICHARD F. STEINBRINK
Collaborator and Friend

Acknowledgments

No one ever writes about the life of a great man without the help of others. It is my great pleasure to thank many who shared their memories with me, and others whose funds of information were of vital importance to me while researching the fascinating life of Dr. Nelson Glueck.

I wish to express my gratitude to Dr. Helen I. Glueck of Cincinnati for her hospitality and friendliness in granting me her time and so many personal facts about her husband's life. My thanks go also to Mr. Harry Glueck of Cincinnati, and Mr. Nathan P. Revel of San Francisco, who allowed me a look into their memories of the childhood of their brother.

Dr. Jacob R. Marcus of the Hebrew Union College–Jewish Institute of Religion, a storyteller and gentleman par excellence, gave me new insights into the youth and career of his good friend.

To Dr. Stanley F. Chyet, also of the College-Institute, I offer thanks for some valuable writing advice.

I thank Mrs. Ruth Frenkel of the College-Institute for her gracious courtesy and the warmth with which she shared some of her recollections of Dr. Glueck with me.

Mrs. Fanny Zelcer and members of her staff at the American Jewish Archives in Cincinnati have my special thanks for assistance promptly and pleasantly rendered.

I appreciate the willingness of Mrs. Eleanor Vogel to reminisce about the years she spent in close collaboration with Dr. Glueck as his archaeological secretary.

To Rabbi and Mrs. David H. Wice of Philadelphia I am grateful for many glimpses into their long personal friendship with Nelson Glueck.

Mrs. Mildred Kurland, librarian of Congregation Rodeph Shalom in Philadelphia, deserves my thanks for providing material, "leads," and kind understanding at all times.

To Dr. Samuel Paley I offer my appreciation for his criticism and suggestions following his reading of the manuscript.

1

It was time to go.

It was a Sunday afternoon in the autumn of 1908, and getting late. Already, from the park bench across the road where he sat waiting, Papa had called him twice.

But Nelson lingered, curious about a glimmering object he had seen protruding from the sand. With a small stick he scratched in the earth, loosening the soil a little, and there it was. It had waited just for him. Dropped on this spot by a hunter, perhaps many centuries ago, it had stayed there, waiting.

"Papa," he cried excitedly, "come look at this. Just look at this beauty."

His father, carrying the basket filled with objects that they had found that day in the Indian mounds at the edge of the city, came over to where the young boy stood. Clutched in Nelson's palm was a pink quartz arrowhead, covered by a few clinging grains of sand. Clearly a prize specimen, Papa agreed at once, an unusually handsome treasure which they must keep for their collection.

A little later, slender, brown-eyed Nelson Glueck stood at the suburban streetcar stop with his father, ready to board the downtown trolley. Still entranced with his special find, he held the quartz against the sky, letting the sinking Ohio sun filter through the stone's wide range of colors, from a cool grayish white to a glowing light red.

What great mysteries of the past the earth held captive.

Nelson's eyes grew even darker as he thought of the people long ago whose arrowhead he had found, who might have held this lustrous stone as he held it now, admiring its natural beauty. What were they like, the people who had carved this quartz? How had they lived? Why had they disappeared?

When they reached Cincinnati's West End, the boy and his father left the trolley and walked home through familiar streets, passing the houses of friends and neighbors on their way. Nelson's imagination was still stirred by the huge earthworks he had just seen. He tried, in the fading light, to blot out the sidewalks and cobblestones of the streets where they walked. Instead he pictured in his mind the area as it might once have looked: woods and fertile farmlands crossed by streams, where the Indian had lived, farmed, worshiped his gods, and been buried long before the white man trod this ground.

Nelson thought of question after question to ask until his father stood still on the sidewalk and said, "You're like a thirsty sponge, Nelson . . . endlessly curious . . . and I don't have all the answers." His father spoke English with a strong Russian accent.

But Nelson knew that his tall, vigorous father was pleased by his many questions, not annoyed as he pretended to be. Not many months ago Nelson's grammar school teacher, Dr. Koch, had asked to speak with Papa. His father had taken the afternoon off to visit the school, and when he came home, his eyes sparkling happily, he had gone into the bedroom to discuss with Mama what had taken place. Nelson wasn't quite sure what his teacher had said, but he knew it couldn't have been too bad, judging by Mama's glances in his direction. Papa told him that Dr. Koch said he was a good student who ought to be encouraged. Just how this was to take place Nelson did not learn. His parents did not discuss such matters in front of the children. But Papa was more amenable to answering questions after his meeting with Dr. Koch, and questions were something Nelson could think up constantly.

Perhaps Papa did not know all the exciting bits of local Indian lore, but he was interested and willing to learn about new things himself. He was Nelson's favorite companion. Morris Glueck was a big man whose legs moved lightly and easily over the rocks and roots of the fossil hill at the lower end of Clifton Avenue. They went there whenever Nelson wanted to gather specimens for his fossil collection, and Papa helped him chip away pieces from the huge exposed boulder, known for its extraordinary fossils, which drew many amateur explorers to the site.

Certainly Papa was pleased with Nelson's eagerness when he found especially interesting chunks of rock imbedded with layers of animal and plant remains. Papa helped Nelson to carry them home. He showed his son how to put together a hobby collection, and Nelson spent hours over it. The boy kept a notebook in which he recorded each find systematically, carefully noting the exact location where he had picked it up and the date on which he found it.

Sometimes Papa looked at him with a curiously faraway expression, and then Nelson knew his father was thinking of his own youth and family in Europe. Perhaps he was wondering then whether his own children would ever measure up to his ancestors, those scholarly rabbis in Lithuania who had devoted their whole lives to learning.

Nelson never tired of hearing about that family of illustrious men, and Morris never tired of telling stories about them.

Morris's maternal grandfather, Rabbi Moshe Yitzchak Revel, of Ponevezh, was the subject of one of the stories.

Rabbi Revel was a man of such learning and stature in his community that his son-in-law, Rabbi Nahum Shraga Finkel, requested—and received—permission to adopt the Revel family name upon his marriage to the famous rabbi's daughter.

Rabbi Nahum Shraga Revel became Morris's father. When Morris was born in 1869 in a suburb of Kovno, Lithuania, he was named in honor of his grandfather, Moshe Yitzchak Revel.

Kovno was at that time a great center of Jewish learning. As Nelson's father often reminded his own children, the Jews of Kovno respected their rabbis and listened to their advice with awed reverence.

Although he knew that both his great-grandfather and his grandfather had been noted Torah scholars, Nelson liked best to hear about his young uncle, Dov (Bernard) Revel. Dov—Morris's half-brother—was the son of Rabbi Nahum Shraga Revel's second wife. Dov was only six years old when he was proclaimed an *illui*, a prodigy, by Kovno's wisest man of learning, Rabbi Isaac Elchanan Spektor.

Papa always said that this was a commendation not easily given. Young Dov possessed an extraordinary photographic memory for talmudic tracts. He could cite any passage by heart after he had once seen it.

"Is it really true that Uncle Bernard was a rabbi at sixteen?" Nelson asked more than once. It was hard to imagine a rabbi hardly older than a boy. The rabbis he knew were old, wise, and bearded.

Morris had already left Lithuania when his half-brother was ordained, but there was proof that some of the country's most famous rabbis had been present to see Dov receive *smicha*, his ordination.

For Morris there had not been time to acquire the rabbinical schooling then available only in Europe. He had left Lithuania as a youngster to avoid the fate of every young man living within the Czar's domain: military service in the Russian army. Since the Revel family name was so well known in Kovno Guberniya, Morris discreetly left it behind. His passport was made out in the new name he had chosen for himself. Moshe Yitzchak Revel was now Morris Glueck, who hoped the German word *Glueck* (good luck) would serve him well.

Life in the American Midwest was totally different from what he had known before, yet Morris Glueck had managed to feel at home quickly in Cincinnati, the town on the Ohio River where he decided to make his start.

If he ever longed for the family and friends he had left behind in Lithuania, these longings were put to rest after he met Anna Ethel Rubin. The beautiful young girl also came from Morris's home district of Kovno Guberniya. From the moment he saw her, Morris knew he would never be homesick again.

Morris and Anna were married in May of 1893 and moved into a small house on Court Street in the heart of the city. There, the following year, the first of their nine children was born.

Two children, a sister, Rachel, and a brother, Nathan, were already in the family when Nelson Glueck was born in Cincinnati on June 4, 1900. The second son of Morris and Anna arrived at the beginning of a new century. His father named him for the spring month of Nissan, a time of renewal.

Later in his life people were often to remark on the strange coincidence of Nelson's birth just a few weeks after the death of Rabbi Isaac Mayer Wise, famous founder of American Reform Judaism, who passed away on March 26, 1900. But as a young child, Nelson knew little outside the orthodox teachings of Judaism.

At home with the traditions of his people, Morris himself gave his children their firm foundation of faith. They learned their prayers easily. In such a household religion came naturally, almost like breathing.

There were other worlds to be found outside the house, and in time Nelson found out about them too. Cincinnati was not only a town producing machinery, automobile parts, soap, and farm tools. It also had a reputation as a dynamic city of culture. It possessed libraries, museums, and concert halls, open to anyone willing to use them. Many of these cultural institutions were founded by Jewish people who had been a part of the heavy German immigration during the middle 1800s. Numbering only fifteen thousand in a population nearly a third of a million strong, Cincinnati's Jews were active in all aspects of the city's life. One Jewish citizen—Julius Fleischmann— even sat in the mayor's seat in the year of Nelson's birth.

The Gluecks, in their modest little house in the immigrant district, were far removed from the financial and civic endeavors of their fellow Jews. Their problems were more personal and pressing.

The truth was that in the large family of Morris Glueck there was never enough money. Morris struggled daily and mightily to feed and clothe his growing youngsters, but he did not have the gift for making money. While others of his generation quickly grew prosperous after their arrival in this country, the little Morris earned as a customer peddler on the streets of Cincinnati he made with great effort and at much physical expense. Some said of him that he never became a well-to-do businessman because his heart was not in selling or trading but in the world of books.

Despite the chronic lack of money, life in the Glueck household was happy. The family grew with the arrival of Sam, Ben, and Harry, followed by the birth of daughters

Esther and Sally. For Morris Glueck his family was his life. When his oldest daughter, Rachel, was twenty-one years old, the youngest child, Hillel, was born.

The highlight of the Glueck family's week came with the setting sun on Friday evenings when the heartbeat of Court Street slowed down.

During the rest of the week Court Street was never quiet. It had a Farmer's Market at one end where traffic was heavy and constant. At the stalls housewives bargained and gossiped with neighbors they met there. Fish sellers, butchers, and produce vendors shouted their wares, and noise pulsed from dawn until the closing hour.

Nelson went to the market often, but he went in the evenings, when his mother sent him to buy up leftover vegetables, cheaper at that late hour. And if the day's business had been good, the vegetable woman threw in an apple for Nelson because she liked the skinny youngster with the large brown eyes.

On Sabbath eve even the sound of playing children was stilled. It was at that hour that Anna Glueck stirred her soup, and the thought of their mother's dinner brought all Gluecks, big or little, home a bit faster.

Anna had strict rules about observing Sabbath laws. All preparations had to be finished before she blessed the candles. For once she had spoken the blessing, no one in her household lifted a hand in work until the festive day had been bid farewell again.

When on Fridays Nelson came home from school, the odor of roasting potatoes and freshly baked challah always met him in the hall. He kissed his mother, who hustled between kitchen and dining room directing her oldest daughter.

"Ready to set the table, Rae?"

Like the aroma of her cooking, Anna's admonitions to her children were her way of greeting the Sabbath. As each of her boys came home, he was hurried into an assigned chore before he changed into the clean clothes he found laid out on the bed. No one complained. Everyone in the family was aware that Anna Glueck had more work than she could handle and needed the help of her children.

Before the Sabbath lamp was lighted, Morris Glueck came home to a house spotlessly tidy, to a dining table set with their best china, and to a family ready to welcome him. Only then would Anna reach for her fringed shawl, cover her head, and kindle the lights in the candlesticks she had brought from Kovno Guberniya as a girl. Her arms weaving in blessing, she murmured the prayer that ushered the peace and joy of the Sabbath into their home.

Morris was happiest on the Sabbath. Surrounded by his children and his wife, who had stayed slim and handsome despite the years and the cares, the tall man with the dark beard felt himself the true king of his household. He looked forward to Saturday morning when he took his sons to *shul*. In the small synagogue of the Orthodox East European congregation to which they belonged, the second pew was reserved for the Gluecks, and no one else sat in it. In this sanctuary Morris was known and respected for his religious scholarship.

Sabbath worship over, he and Anna sat on the front porch of their house, greeting afternoon visitors from the neighborhood who called on them, wished them a good day, or drew on Morris's experience for a bit of advice.

Morris felt pride when he saw that his children had absorbed his teachings. Along with the rituals he instilled his profound love of Judaism into all his sons and daughters. That he was successful showed in the joy with which they celebrated the Sabbath and the festivals—a joy in being together, among each other.

True, the walls of their little house witnessed enough squabbles and brotherly fights, but wasn't that normal with such a healthy, strapping bunch?

No, Morris often told himself, even without money the Gluecks were truly a rich family.

2

IT WAS OBVIOUS to his parents and to the older children that Nelson knew early what he wanted and was fiercely determined to get ahead in life.

Easily the most studious of the Glueck children, he never needed to be told when and how to study. He had an easy confidence that enough hard work and persistence would accomplish for him all he set out to do.

It awed the family a bit when Nelson tried to find a quiet study nook in the midst of their crowded, noisy household with its good-natured clamor. But he always found one. Nelson learned early in his youth to concentrate on what he wanted to do without letting anything distract him. Many a midnight his older brother, Nathan, arriving home from an ushering job at the Cincinnati opera, found Nelson sitting at the kitchen table so intent on his homework that he did not hear the front door open and close.

Seeing his father tired and spent after a day of trudging from one customer to the next, and realizing how little Papa's labors accomplished, Nelson knew he would not want to go into business. Already he had had a taste of what it was to walk the pavement trying to earn a few coins.

At thirteen he had become a newspaper boy. The residential area where he delivered his papers after school was a long way from home. Although his long, sturdy legs

10

took to the work easily, he soon learned that he would not get rich selling newspapers. He sympathized with his father, for he suspected that just like Morris he also did not have the gift for making money.

Once they were old enough, all the Glueck children held down afterschool jobs to pay for the extras they needed. Papa did well to feed and clothe them. Four times a year each Glueck child received a new outfit. Every boy was bought new trousers and a jacket, a shirt and socks to match. When the girls giggled with pleasure over a new dress and petticoat, Morris beamed. It was important to him that his children knew the satisfaction of being well dressed. It made him feel he was a good provider. As long as he could work, his children would have a home. He would support them through their high school days, but if they wanted to go to college they had to work their way themselves.

Though the Gluecks knew they could not finance the education of a scholar, Morris and Anna became uneasy when they thought about their second son's future. Even without the prompting of Dr. Koch they had known that in this youngster the gift for learning ought to be furthered. How would they do it?

Nelson did not express any early decision about what he wanted to be. There was much to be learned in this world, and he wanted to study as much of it as he could.

Did he want to become a rabbi like his uncle?

Morris's younger brother, Dov, Americanized as Bernard, had been living in New York since 1906. Continuing a spectacular scholastic career, Dov had already acquired an outstanding reputation as a Jewish scholar. Now, in 1915, Bernard Revel had just been asked to head the Rabbi Isaac Elchanan Theological Seminary in New York, training school for traditionally Orthodox rabbis. Morris was very proud of his brother.

"Hardly a yeshiva is left in Europe that can operate normally. What will happen if war comes? Where will the new generation of rabbis come from, if not right here in this country?"

Morris looked around at his sons scraping away at the remnants of Anna's dinner on their plates.

"Who knows," he smiled, "perhaps we can count on a future rabbi right here at this table, maybe."

But Anna shook her head. "I doubt you'll make an Orthodox rabbi out of any of these. Besides, how can we afford to send a boy all the way to New York to school?"

But Nelson had private thoughts about his future. One Friday night after dinner he walked into the dining room and found his father alone. Morris was sitting at the table with books scattered around him, reading by the light of the Sabbath candles.

"Papa, can we talk?"

Morris lifted his head and nodded. With one hand he invited Nelson to sit. Hesitatingly, Nelson brought up the subject of his studies.

He admired Uncle Bernard very much, he said. He wanted to be like him and study a lot. But he wanted to study history and science.

"They're good subjects, but why does a rabbi need science?"

"That's why we need to talk, Papa. I don't want to be a rabbi. I would not be happy as a rabbi. And I wouldn't like going to a school where they tell me I cannot study a subject because it isn't meant for a pious Jew to learn about it."

Morris rose from the table and started walking up and down the room in silence. He was a modern man, despite his traditional background. He knew that none of his other children had Nelson's intense desire for learning. He had foreseen that the spark he detected in his son would have to be fostered differently than he had hoped.

"I, too, have been thinking about it, son," he said, standing still near the window. "Your mother and I have talked about it, and we have decided the training at the Hebrew Union College may suit you best. Perhaps you would like to take courses there when you enter high school?"

Everyone knew about the excellent teachers over at the College, well-trained liberal scholars of renown. But for Papa, with his Orthodox upbringing and strict observance of Judaism, to suggest that a Reform school might have advantages over a yeshiva, that took understanding and foresight.

"Papa, I . . ." but Morris waved him to silence and motioned him to come over to the window.

"If you want to be a scholar, that's all right with me. But then we must make certain you get the best training."

Together they stood at the window, peering through a crack in Anna's starched curtains at dark Court Street outside. Nelson felt warm and protected with Papa's arm around his shoulders.

When, on a balmy spring evening in 1915, Nelson and his father hurried up the stone steps to the Gothic entrance of Hebrew Union College, the school had stood barely two years on its Clifton Avenue hilltop.

Just like Reform Judaism in America, the school had grown remarkably since the October day in 1875 when Rabbi Isaac Mayer Wise of Cincinnati took over the religious training of fourteen boys who met in the basement of Bene Israel Temple. With one assistant to help him teach an assorted group of thirteen-year-olds, Rabbi Wise was spreading the growth of a new branch of Judaism.

Born in Germany, the Jewish Reform movement came

about through political changes in the status of the Jew and through the growth of the new physical sciences, which looked at the teachings of the Bible in a critical, analytic fashion.

With the emancipation of the Jew into a full citizen of the countries in which he lived came the desire to become more like the non-Jewish citizens of these countries. Certain changes in the life-style of the former member of the ghetto community were necessary if he was to adapt himself to the laws and customs of the land which now accepted him as an equal. Among these changes were allowing the use of the vernacular instead of an all-Hebrew service, permitting worshipers to ride to services, the use of organ music to enhance the beauty of religious services, modifying mourning customs which no longer applied in the modern age, and establishing a greater amount of religious equality for women.

The impact of modern science on Bible criticism resulted, in the case of Reform Judaism, in the belief that the Bible, though not physically written by the hand of God, was still the repository of divine ideas which served as man's greatest source of inspiration and instruction.

Reform Judaism rejected the coming of the Messiah, another traditional tenet. Instead it adopted the belief that the true Messianic Age will have come when all nations practice truth, justice, and peace.

With these basic beliefs Rabbi Isaac Mayer Wise, along with others, hoped to unite a new kind of Jew to a new kind of world, frontier America. In 1873 he persuaded twenty-eight delegates of American Reform congregations to form a Union of American Hebrew Congregations. The first big objective of the Union was also Wise's dearest wish—to establish a rabbinical seminary.

From the basement schoolroom to a private house to the hilltop location with two new beautiful buildings,

Rabbi Wise's school became Hebrew Union College, training center for all future American Reform rabbis.

Breathless from the steep slope on Clifton Avenue, Morris paused a moment at the front door, letting his eyes roam over the spacious grounds of the College. He had cut his working day short today, believing he had a reason even more important than making a living.

"Ready?" he asked his son, who stood tall and expectantly beside him.

"Yes," answered Nelson. His hand was already on the door handle.

Together they walked into the entrance hall. Ahead of them double doors led to the College chapel. Finding the chapel deserted at this hour, father and son turned left in the corridor and headed for the stairs to the second-floor classrooms. Upstairs they were directed to the room where Dr. Gotthard Deutsch taught his students. Now only a few young men lingered near the front of the classroom, packing up books and papers. Father and son stood in the back of the room, waiting.

"Mr. Glueck?" The voice boomed with a strong German accent, pronouncing the name with the German umlaut rather than "Glick," the way most people did. Professor Deutsch sat behind a massive desk, looking, with his long white beard and a wreath of strong white hair, like one of the biblical prophets whose pictures hung on the classroom walls.

Morris walked forward. "My son Nelson," he introduced, shaking hands with the professor, who had risen from his chair.

"So this is the young man?" Dr. Deutsch sat down again, studying Nelson with penetrating blue eyes.

Nelson stood in front of the desk looking straight at the older man. He was not frightened by the interview.

"We've come to see about getting my son into your class," Morris began.

Professor Deutsch, his eyes still on Nelson, suddenly remembered to invite the Gluecks to sit down.

"Let me see . . . you wrote he is a good student . . ." His large hands roamed over the desk and pulled out a letter. Silently he reread Morris's letter in their presence. His glasses slipped over his nose as he read.

"He is a very good student. He is an ambitious boy, eager to learn," Morris said when the professor had finished reading. His voice was anxious.

"How old are you, young man?" Dr. Deutsch addressed Nelson directly.

"Fifteen, sir, by the time the next high school term starts."

"And you wish to study philosophy and Jewish history with us?"

"Yes, sir."

The setting sun fell through the high windows behind Dr. Deutsch's chair and lit on the glass of a framed map of the Holy Land. Nelson had a strong urge to follow the direction of the sunbeam and look at the map, but he resisted it. There would be time for that after he was officially admitted to this classroom.

Dr. Deutsch had an enviable reputation as a scholar and a teacher. From what Papa said, Nelson would be fortunate to become a student of his. From what Nelson had heard, Dr. Deutsch was feared by his students as a strict disciplinarian. Nelson sat quietly in his chair.

"Take him in hand, sir," Morris pleaded. "This is a boy who needs to be directed. I think you will be satisfied with him. He will learn fast."

Looking more than ever like a painting of a patriarch, Dr. Deutsch stood up and walked out from behind his desk. Again he held out his hand to Morris.

"I think you're right, Mr. Glueck. With such a family as yours, your son should make a good student. I will take him for the fall term," his loud voice announced.

"Thank you, Professor," Morris pumped his hand vigorously. "You've made a good choice."

Nelson pushed back his chair, waiting to tell Professor Deutsch goodbye. His eyes strayed to the map on the wall at last. Soon he would be able to study it more closely.

Nelson started high school that fall. His family, following the general exodus of the Jewish population from downtown Cincinnati, had moved. They now lived in "hilltop" Avondale, a residential section of tree-lined streets and stone houses.

By the end of each school day Nelson had walked at least three miles from his home to the high school to Hebrew Union College and back home. He enjoyed his walks through the pleasantly shaded streets, for this was the only exercise he had on these long school days, which lasted from 8:30 in the morning until 6:30 in the evening.

The heavy school program put an end to delivering newspapers, and Nelson felt the constant pinch for money more keenly now. He had outgrown the days when he and his brothers ran a lemonade stand at the Farmer's Market during the summers, passing the franchise on to the younger boys in the family. As a teenager he worked in a boys' camp as counselor, loving sports as much as his charges did.

The days flowed into each other, long days spent at school, evenings of studying in preparation for the next day. At home he still searched out a little oasis for himself, trying to find silence in the turbulent household. When that didn't work, he studied in the library at Hebrew Union College, where he worked in the evenings.

More and more Nelson found himself within his own

world now. It was a world of learning and discovery, which occupied him so completely that at times the world in which he lived, the "real" world, seemed miles away.

April 6, 1917 began like every other day except that it was the beginning of Passover.

The Glueck children always looked forward to holidays celebrated in the home, not only because of the pleasant interruption of work or school, but also because of Anna's special holiday dinners.

Nelson, happy that his afternoon class at Hebrew Union College was canceled, went straight home from high school that day. Though it was spring, the trees were barely budding and there was a chill in the air. It seemed to Nelson that more people than usual were in the streets, some bunched in small groups.

When he reached a main intersection Nelson saw a crowd of people around the newspaper stand on the corner. Curious to find out the reason for this gathering, Nelson approached it. Fastened to the top of the news-stand with clothespins was a copy of the afternoon paper. Its front page was covered by just one black word.

He hurried home, and Anna's red-rimmed eyes told him she had already heard the news. Though their Seder would begin shortly, the house was silent of its usual pre-holiday sounds. Everyone moved carefully to avoid making noise, even the little ones, who did not know the reason for their mother's crying.

Morris came home carrying a copy of the newspaper. His shoulders drooped more than Nelson ever remembered. Morris kissed them all, hugging the youngest children and being especially gentle with Anna, whose tears started anew. Nelson had heard them talk often lately about the fate of the East European Jews. He knew that his mother's tears and his father's worry-drawn expression were caused by anxiety over their close relatives still living in Russian-occupied Lithuania.

They read their way through the Haggadah that night with everyone taking parts as usual. Papa hid the Afikomen and rewarded the finder with a bag of candies after dinner. But their singing lacked the usual joy, and even Anna's matzah ball soup did not revive their spirits. All felt relieved when the Seder meal was finally over. Despite the festival of freedom, no one could really be happy on the day America entered the World War.

The map of the Holy Land which so fascinated Nelson during his interview with Dr. Deutsch became very familiar in the three years that he was an afternoon student at the College. Nelson stood in front of it often, sometimes tracing with his finger the outline of the countries he read about in the Bible. The kingdoms of Edom and Moab, Ammon and Gilead, and their once fierce and mighty rulers interested him. Those lands were only a name on the map now. The exact location of their boundaries had been lost for thousands of years.

Wastelands in the desert, that's what remained of the land once occupied by the powerful neighbors of the Israelites. What had they been like in their prime years when the earth had bloomed for them?

During these three years Nelson became intensely interested in the Bible. Like others in his class, he learned that the Bible was a series of recollections transmitted by word of mouth through generations. When descendants of the original narrators finally wrote the stories down, they carefully edited them into purposeful object lessons. Each story illustrated a facet of the relationship between man and God.

Fascinated by the historical facts behind these stories, Nelson became even more absorbed by the ideas they expressed. He understood that these ideas had shown mankind the road to civilization. He wondered about the fact that all the prophecies and commandments which linked people to their God and to each other had begun in that area of the world to which his eyes strayed whenever he found time to raise his head in class.

These were strong ideas. *The sanctity of life* could not have meant much to tribes that offered human sacrifices to their many gods. *Peace* never existed among the countless kingdoms constantly warring with each other. *Brotherhood among men* was unattainable for the people of the desert, who could not trust one another.

As Nelson became more familiar with the life of Moses, he tried to understand why the Exodus took so many years. He became dazzled by descriptions of the Solomonic empire, and found himself completely engrossed by the interchange between historical fact and ideas.

It was mind-stretching stuff, and it appealed to a youngster who had always asked questions. Now he found even more to ask. Why was it this particular spot on earth that had given birth to the major religions? Why had it been the inhabitants of this particular area who were receptive to ideas which would influence the whole Western world?

He did not understand all he learned, but he knew these were subjects of vital interest to him. The little boy who had once pondered over his Indian artifacts was now a young man who wondered about the "background" of the ideas he found in the Bible.

It pleased Morris enormously to see Nelson taking Holy Writ so seriously. Another scholar in the family? There seemed no doubt about it now.

On a June day in 1918 all the Gluecks gathered together proudly to see Nelson receive his Bachelor of Hebrew Literature degree at Hebrew Union College.

In his quiet, modest manner, Nelson was pleased too, but for him this was only the first step on a long road. His appetite was whetted by all the learning that still lay ahead. Already Nelson looked forward to the fall, when he would begin classes at the university.

3

ONLY A FEW BLOCKS away from the familiar campus of Hebrew Union College, down on Clifton Avenue, Nelson's two years of undergraduate study at the University of Cincinnati were to change his whole life. Spellbound, the young man sat through a series of courses which unlocked the science of archaeology to him.

An archaeologist is a student of the past who learns about ancient people through the objects they have left behind. But it is only in the last one hundred years that an important change has come about in the goals of archaeology. It has become a precise science.

Before this change took place, men who searched out the past were motivated by hopes of personal gain. They looked for treasures of gold or valuable statuary which could be sold to museums or private collectors.

Today archaeologists seek out a different treasure. They undertake scientific expeditions hoping to find clues to the past which will fill in the blank pages of history.

Studies at the classics department of the University of Cincinnati were concentrated on the archaeology of Greece and the Orient. Its famous director, Professor Carl Blegen, was an active archaeologist who organized and led expeditions to prehistoric sites. There he excavated, and identified the civilizations he had unearthed from the relics and artifacts he found beneath the soil.

Professor Blegen was an expert in Greek archaeology,

22

and his specialty was the exploration of legendary Troy.

Nelson, like every other schoolboy, had struggled with the epic poems by the great Greek writer, Homer. He knew about Troy, legendary kingdom of ancient heroes and site of the Trojan War.

Homer's *Iliad* and *Odyssey* had for centuries shaped man's knowledge of early Greek history, but nobody had taken these two poems as seriously as a German merchant by the name of Heinrich Schliemann, who made it his life's ambition to uncover the actual site where he believed Homer's heroes had lived, loved, and fought to the death.

In 1871 Schliemann followed his dream. He gathered a work force of native laborers and began digging in western Turkey, at a site which he thought to be the right spot. To his amazement Schliemann found something there. Not only one, but seven strata of civilization were uncovered by his men. One of them had to be the real Troy, the place where Paris had taken the beautiful Helen, a kidnapping which had allegedly set off the great war between the Trojans and the Greeks.

By following the literal truth as he found it in the pages of Homer's poems, Heinrich Schliemann became one of the early archaeologists of world renown. Through his work he had proved that myths and legends, older than written history, often carried an important kernel of facts down through the ages.

For Nelson's inquisitive mind these adventurous tales were like a favorite food. He devoured it, looking all the while for more. He attended his classes, read all he could find, and still did not get enough. In daydreams he saw himself on expeditions, searching out the soil for answers to his ever-present questions, discovering new chapters in the story of man.

The lure of the faraway was always with him. It

appealed strongly to his restless imagination. It had begun with a child's interest in the relics of Indians. Where would his search lead?

The example of Schliemann pursuing his mystical Troy became etched in Nelson's memory. It stayed with him after he finished his classes at the university and followed him into the halls of the Hebrew Union College when he enrolled there as a rabbinical student.

It was in the class of Dr. Julian Morgenstern that he discovered how right he was to have come to Hebrew Union College. Dr. Morgenstern was an outstanding biblical scholar who knew how to stir his students to appreciate their heritage. He was a tough, strict teacher who demanded accuracy and disciplined performance. As a reward his students received his priceless interpretations and commentaries on the books of the Bible.

With his double interest in the history of biblical ideas and in the young science of archaeology, Nelson listened to Dr. Morgenstern's lectures with increasing purpose.

From his reading he came to believe that early scholars with an interest in exploring the Holy Land had been right to think of the Bible as a guidebook to the past. Even if the countries and the peoples mentioned in its pages were gone, there were road markers that pointed the way back. The geographical data had to be true. If only he could see for himself . . .

Not all was seriousness and learning in those student days. Like the aquamarine, his birthstone, Nelson possessed a glittering charm and a clear frankness which made him many friends among both students and faculty.

Nelson was a friend of Sheldon Blank and Walter Rothstein, both of them young men who had much in common with him. The trio daily walked the main streets of Avondale on their familiar route to the College and back, discussing the exciting future just ahead of them. All three would be ordained at the same time, all three were planning to advance their studies in Europe immediately afterward.

Already Nelson had formed a lasting friendship with Jacob Rader Marcus—Jake, as his friends called him—a young history instructor at the College. Unusually bright and articulate, Marcus was an ordained graduate of the College and had been retained to teach future generations of undergraduates. It was as teacher and student that Jake and Nelson had first met.

The shining moment in the chapel came at last. On a warm June day in 1923 Nelson stood before Dr. Morgenstern and by his touch upon his shoulder—the "laying on of hands"—became "Rabbi Glueck." It was for Nelson a proud satisfaction to receive *smicha* from the man from whom he learned so much and who agreed with Nelson that his twin interests would do well in the field of biblical archaeology.

As part of the ceremony, Dr. Morgenstern announced the awarding of a brand-new grant to one of the graduates. As recipient of the first Morgenthau Traveling Fellowship, Nelson Glueck would do postgraduate work at the European university of his choice.

Like the Three Musketeers of the famous French novel, the three young Americans set out in the fall of 1923 to conquer the academic fields of postwar Europe. Sheldon Blank, Walter Rothstein, and Nelson Glueck left Cincinnati's Reading Road behind and sailed for Germany. Though they had recently acquired the dignified status of rabbinical ordination, little about them suggested that these three were clergymen on their way to higher learning.

In his first delirious burst of joy after their arrival in

Berlin, Nelson engaged a horsedrawn *droshke* to drive him and his companions down the wide, tree-planted avenues of the German capital. Only with difficulty did his friends prevent Nelson from yelling "Yippee" at every passerby on the street corners. His elation was boundless. This was his "grand tour," and he intended to make the most of it.

Before he settled down to another season of university classes, Nelson took a good long look at this new world. He enjoyed all he saw. Away from home, heady with his new freedom, he was in no hurry to work, especially since his scholarship covered necessary expenses.

It was refreshing to see how his German counterparts lived. Nelson was impressed with the life-style of the German student—the debating societies, the fraternal organizations, the beer drinking. How different this was from the way he had obtained his schooling. Perhaps he and his two companions ought to try it too. But before all three went too far astray, the voice of conscience stopped them.

The voice of conscience belonged to—of all people— Jake Marcus, who was in Germany at the same time, working on his doctorate. Marcus caught up with the Cincinnati trio in Kiel and saw at one glance that they were having far too good a time.

Was this the way serious scholars behaved, he wanted to know. Had they forgotten the purpose of their stay in Europe?

Sheepishly the three young men agreed that Jacob Marcus was right. They should be working harder. But now that they had had their fun, it would be easier to return to their studies. They would immediately go back to the university courses for which they had signed up.

After the fashion of European university students, Nelson went from school to school seeking out special professors, rather than concentrating on one university. During his first year in Germany he spent time at the University of Berlin, where a famous teacher, Hugo Gressmann, lectured on Palestine, its history, culture, and civilizations.

Often, during his Berlin days, he visited the home of Dr. Leo Baeck, where he met other rabbis and scholars from all over the world. Even then Dr. Baeck was famous. He was the rabbi of a large Berlin congregation, a scholar and writer. He lectured at the liberal Academy for the Study of Judaism. In time Rabbi Leo Baeck would be the leader who guided the Jews of Germany through one of the darkest periods in their history, yet already in these earlier days he enriched his listeners by his sermons and lectures. Nelson remembered those Sunday afternoons at the Baeck home affectionately as hours of great warmth and stimulation.

From Berlin Nelson went to Heidelberg and attended its university. Here another famous scholar, Professor Willi Staerk, was known for his work on the background of biblical writings.

Nelson had one great asset during his days at the German universities. The dual language system of his Cincinnati schooling had given him such a firm grounding in the German language that he had no difficulty following lectures or reading his assignments. It was almost natural for him to think in German. Since almost all the scientific research material available was written in German, his childhood language training proved a blessing.

At the third school he attended, the University of Jena, he decided on the dissertation he would write for his doctoral degree. There was no question in what language it would be.

In 1927 Nelson's thesis, "The Word 'Grace' in Old Testament Usage," was accepted by the University of

Jena. Far away from home and family, he became Nelson Glueck, Doctor of Philosophy.

Originally he had planned to expand the thesis. He wanted to make it the first chapter in a book. It was part of his interest in the history of biblical ideas which had been so important to him as a student at the Hebrew Union College. But he grew tired of the cloistered shelter of university libraries. His restless mind was not content to stay with just one project alone. His sense of adventure sought more direct, involved action. What precisely this would be, he still did not know.

Despite the pleasure of reading about the work that interested him, he suddenly wondered why he was sitting in Germany, examining endless volumes. Was this the true work of a biblical archaeologist? And how could it take place outside of Palestine?

Years later he explained in his own words what had moved him toward the next important step in his life: "I felt it necessary to learn more about the lands in which the Bible had its roots and about the civilizations and peoples reflected in its pages than was possible to ascertain from extant literature. The only additional source of information was literally in the soil of the Holy Land and of neighboring countries, and the only way to obtain it, was, using the modern colloquialism, to dig it."

Exhilarated as he was at the thought of traveling to Palestine, Nelson was also practical enough to ask himself: what am I looking for? How will I recognize what I find?

It was clear that he lacked concise scientific training. Looking around for an expert teacher who could give him that training, Nelson had little difficulty deciding on the man under whom he wished to study.

In the late summer of 1927 Nelson packed his bags and bid Berlin goodbye. This time he knew his journey would bring him closer to his goal.

4

O<small>NLY</small> A FEW HOURS after arriving in Jerusalem that warm and glowing autumn of 1927, Nelson fell in love—with the City of David. He was a man seeing his dream come true, and when he toured all the landmarks he had read about, each one greeted him like an old friend. It was a love affair that would last a lifetime.

Soon afterwards he paid his first visit to the American School of Oriental Research just outside the walls of the Old City. He did not know it then, but that first friendly handshake with the school's director, William Foxwell Albright, marked the start of his career as an archaeologist.

The world's foremost biblical archaeologist was still a young man, almost too young for his enormous reputation. Building on the work of previous giants in the field of archaeology, Dr. Albright had established a new system of classifying pottery. This unique dating system had opened the way to scientific excavation of historical ruins throughout Palestine. It was a simple, highly accurate code which allowed a quick dating of all new finds, and even artifacts from past excavations could be dated more precisely with it.

Palestine is dotted with the graveyards of innumerable civilizations, most of them in the form of hillocks called tells (from the Hebrew word *tell*, meaning "mound"). Fortunately for the archaeologist, these ruins abound with potsherds, the broken fragments of ancient pottery, uncovered either by the natural force of erosion or by the inquisitive hands of man.

Nelson, in his book *The Other Side of the Jordan*, describes how a tell is formed.

> In the course of time, the first village built on top of a hill, and surrounded by a fortification-wall, would be destroyed, either by an earthquake, or by a fire which may have broken out accidentally or as the result of an enemy attack. When, sometime after the destruction of the first village, another group of people wanted to build another village in its place, they would be compelled by the very conditions which determined the location of the first village, to build the second one on exactly the same place . . .
>
> The practice of thus building one village upon the ruins of the preceding one led in the course of time to the formation of an entire artificial city-hill, within which might be concealed the ruins of five or ten more villages or cities built one on top of another. When such a hill of destroyed cities was finally abandoned, even the houses of the topmost and last city having been overthrown and covered by debris, it became known as a *tell*. . . . Such a tell may be likened to a small skyscraper, each city in it being comparable to a separate floor.

As one generation succeeded another, destroyed by natural causes or by a war, a wealth of artifacts remained behind. Of these, climatic conditions decayed everything except some architecture, bone or stone tools, and the intensely fired and baked pieces of clay pottery. Pottery is one of the few lasting materials to survive history, sometimes the only one visible to be found above

the ground. Devastating earthquakes, destructive warfare, and changes of temperature have come and gone. As
Nelson was to discover for himself, "Pottery is man's most
enduring material. Wood disappears, stone crumbles,
glass decays, metal corrodes. Only pottery lasts forever."

Pottery, then, became one key to the past. From the
time Near East people first contained their substances of
life in vessels of earthenware, molded of clay and fired in
intense heat—jugs for bringing water from wells, bowls
for cooking food, jars to store grain against the future—
pottery has accompanied them throughout the ages. This
same pottery has provided a relatively accurate key to the
archaeologist searching out the past.

Even if the pottery had shattered and only the broken
shards remained, a competent archaeologist, trained in
Dr. Albright's dating system, could locate the place in
time in which the pottery had originated. His clue? Each
civilization had contributed its own style of pottery,
unique to it alone. The skilled eye of the archaeologist
recognized that civilization and its place in time, and
could thus determine the age of the ruin where the
pottery had been found.

Albright had matched pottery to items with positively
fixed dates, such as the records of Egyptian kings, coins,
or inscriptions, and produced a highly accurate cross-
index. A potsherd which had definite characteristics, such
as a rim, brim, bare handle, or contained decoration,
could be tested against this index and identified in an
almost foolproof manner.

At a time when archaeology was not yet an accurate
science, many glaring mistakes had been made in the
dating of ruins throughout Palestine. Thus, crusader
castles were identified as the fortifications of King David,
and structures of late Moslem origin were ascribed to the
Romans. Because they did not know how to use the clues

provided by the ever-present pottery, early archaeologists simply overlooked them. And sometimes they
just refused to use knowledge already published by
other men, being a very human breed and concerned with
personal glory.

To Nelson the Albright system seemed eminently
practical and suitable for the work he wanted to do. The
scientific, clear-cut dating method appealed to him. It
cleared away the cobwebs of romantic guessing that had
for so long clung to archaeology and made research into
the past precise and definite.

Fascinated by this detective work into history, Nelson
took up his new job as Dr. Albright's apprentice with his
typical determination and energy. Luckily he was in the
right place at the proper time and could satisfy his drive to
master the pottery system.

The American School of Oriental Research was not a
large institution but was well known among scholars.
From its Jerusalem headquarters on Saladin Road it did
extremely important work in archaeology. When the
school did not have funds to mount expeditions of its own,
its staff worked as consultants with other archaeologists on
major excavations. During the time of Nelson's apprenticeship, Professor Albright directed a major project, the
excavation of Tell Beit Mirsim, near Hebron.

In the early Palestinian dawn Nelson awoke, stung by a
flea which had penetrated the tightly rolled blanket in
which he slept. That he was to be a favorite target of all the
vermin in the desert was already evident. Scratching the
bites on his arm, swollen from insect poison, he felt as
if every flea in the Near East had determined to torture
him. Hearing a movement in the tent, he turned to see
another student archaeologist slap his leg in his sleep and
turn over. So he was not alone. Only the chief, Professor

Albright, lay on his cot in peaceful slumber, unaware of the small creatures tormenting his companions during their much-needed rest.

Shivering from the early morning cold, Nelson decided to get up. It would soon be reveille anyway. Shortly the whole camp would rise to face another day of discoveries while battling the sun around the clock.

Squinting in the semi-darkness he barely made out the typewritten sheet pinned to the tent wall by Dr. Albright. During this dig, which would last from May to October, he already knew what was expected of him. But the sheet reminded him and the rest of the staff how much hard work actually lay ahead.

DAILY WORK SCHEDULE

4:15 A.M.	Rising bell
4:30 A.M.	First breakfast
5:00 to 8:30 A.M.	Work
8:30 A.M.	Second breakfast
9:00 A.M.	Work
11:00 A.M.	Break for rest
11:15 A.M.	Work
12:30 P.M.	Lunch
1:30 to 4:00 P.M.	Free time
4:00 to 5:30 P.M.	Cleaning, mending, cataloging

All staff members are on call for various odd jobs

5:30 to 6:30 P.M.	Consultation or lecture
7:00 to 8:00 P.M.	Dinner
7:45 to 8:45 P.M.	Lecture
9:00 P.M.	Lights out

Looking from his tent flap into the veiled purplish haze hiding from view the two Arab villages on either side of the tell, Nelson breathed deeply of the pure morning air. The world felt newly born here. And yet he knew otherwise. To the north of the excavation, amid the terraced vineyards and the well-cultivated fruit orchards, sat Hebron, the ancient Israelite capital where David had been crowned king.

And only a few yards from where he stood, deep archaeological trenches criss-crossed the earth, reminders that beneath the many levels of debris they had uncovered lay proof that man had struggled here since before the recording of history.

Tell Beit Mirsim was the site of an ancient Israelite walled town that had seen continued human occupation from the thirteenth century B.C.E. to Babylonian times. Biblical scholars believed it to be the site of the town of Debir, mentioned as having been burned down by Joshua in his campaign to invade and settle Canaan.

Tell Beit Mirsim was not the first archaeological dig Nelson had seen. During this first year in Palestine he had visited other excavations throughout the land. Palestine resembled a beehive of at least two dozen mounds under attack by archaeologists' hoes and picks, for teams from numerous countries were at work here, digging out cities whose names had long been forgotten, except as references in the Bible.

Though not the largest or the most important Palestinian dig, Tell Beit Mirsim had a special appeal to the scientists and student volunteers who worked in its depths. It was clear to them that few archaeologists in the world could eclipse the scholarly methods and the integrity of the man who led them in this excavation. They admired the skill with which Dr. Albright and his associates recovered the artifacts found at Tell Beit Mirsim, studied and identified them, and then—through their publication—made them available to scientists everywhere.

Professor Albright was a top scientist. Nelson, working with him day after day, felt a special spiritual bond to his teacher. He knew Dr. Albright as a deeply religious man who, as the son of a Methodist minister, knew the Bible as few other living men knew it. With him there was no conflict between science and religion, for he did not seek to "prove" the Bible. He accepted it fully and firmly. As an archaeologist he sought to discover the history of man, and the Bible turned out to be an amazingly accurate road map. For Nelson his teacher's views became lifelong lessons in objective scientific truth.

Someday, Nelson knew, he would conduct his own dig. For his own future use he absorbed carefully all he saw in the daily activities at Tell Beit Mirsim. Already he had learned that a successful dig was conducted like a military campaign, regimented and arduous.

Most excavations were sponsored by universities or learned societies, so an important aim of the expedition was to find new acquisitions for the museum shelves of their sponsor.

Because most expeditions were led by professors and student volunteers on sabbatical vacations from their schools, the short time usually available limited them.

Nelson's most important lesson came in studying the men who made up the professional staff of the dig. These were the heart of a dig. Their competence, knowledge, and specialized skills determined the accomplishment of the excavation; their discoveries filled in the blank pages in the story of mankind.

Without a capable *administrator* no excavation project could function. It was he who specialized in salaries, work schedules, and housing arrangements. He made the payroll, kept the accounts, and wrote the necessary letters.

The *chief archaeologist* headed the campaign, usually with the help of one assistant for the general archaeological work. An *architect,* who surveyed sites and drew the plans from which the expedition worked, was as necessary as the *photographer,* who took pictures of the location and of each find. Every dig was self-destructive: with each shovelful of dirt brought to the surface the original site shrank. Artifacts broke during unearthing or cleaning, some objects fell apart when exposed to air. Photographs often remained the only witness to their existence.

The rising bell rang. In a few minutes there was movement within the tents. Soon men stepped outside, stretched, greeted their neighbors and the morning. Tell Beit Mirsim was once more filled with excitement and the tension of a new day with the chance of important discoveries. Everyone in this camp had been brought here in search of missing pieces in the puzzle of the past. Perhaps this day would bring them closer to their goal.

Tell Beit Mirsim became Nelson's classroom. The baskets filled with pottery shards were his textbooks.

Lovingly his hand rubbed a tiny clay juglet he had gently lifted from the straw basket just brought in by the excavation's Arab foreman. He felt he learned something new from every specimen. He scrutinized each piece for thickness, color, and design, then compared it to other shards on the laboratory shelves at the American School. He was beginning to learn how pieces could be fitted back together into their original shape, and from the reconstruction he could tell whether the object had once been a bowl, a vase, or an urn.

He pulled out an excavation card, set the juglet down before him, and wrote in what information he had about the pottery. Numbered excavation cards, used to catalogue each item as it was unearthed, were the permanent dossiers of each item found in a dig. On them all known data was recorded: the level at which the object was found, a drawing of it—done to scale, the estimated time of its origin, and a word description. This was the last step in the long process of notetaking which began with log books, lists, and descriptions of find places.

Under Dr. Albright's expert direction Nelson had become skilled at recognizing the shapes and designs of vessels. The geometric, floral, or animal pattern with which an ancient potter had embellished his handiwork often provided the clue to its origin.

This little clay vessel had once been a cosmetic container. Nelson judged it might have held kohl, the eye makeup women used to enhance their looks. As he flicked a camel's-hair brush over the clinging sand particles, he reflected that, thanks to his excellent training, he had come a long way from his beginnings as a novice to whom all pieces of clay looked similar.

Not only could he identify the vessel's age and, from its decoration, guess at the people who made it, but he also knew that the kohl once held in this tiny red clay pot had traveled from a faraway country. The woman who hoped to improve her beauty with the contents of the juglet must have lived during days when foreign trade was possible.

Gently he replaced the earthenware vessel, now wearing its identifying catalogue card, in the basket destined to travel to the American School in Jerusalem. Each object in the basket had a story to tell. Each was a clue left behind by ancient men and women, revealing their habits, their way of life, and the infinitesimal part they had played along the slow, long trek of history.

At the end of the 1928 season at Tell Beit Mirsim, Nelson decided to go home. He had mastered many phases of the pottery knowledge, and Dr. Albright was highly pleased with him. He was certain that the young man would make a fine archaeologist for he possessed two absolute requirements of the profession: stamina and painstaking persistence.

But Nelson had been abroad for five years as a student, and now he felt he ought to earn a steady income. He thought he could do this better in America than in Palestine.

Leaving Palestine after it had become such an important part of his life and work was painful. The consolation for it was the arrangement he had made with Dr. Albright: he would return for another season with the American School the following summer. Since Palestinian winters were not especially suited for excavations, Nelson might as well wait to continue his field experience during the rainless summer months.

He had not realized how painful it would be to leave them behind—the school, his teacher, and above all, the land. The Judean hills circling Jerusalem, those flat-topped mounds in the desert waiting to yield their history, the fertile greenery of the ancient Jordan Valley.

Once he had had a vague, unfocused dream. It was born during his student days when his eyes roamed longingly over the map of the Holy Land. The dream was still his but now he had more. He had tools with which he could seek out those hilly kingdoms of Moab, Edom, and Ammon and all the other shadowy places beckoning to him. He knew now he would find them. All he had to do was to follow the descriptions written down in the Bible.

5

Nelson's homecoming was joyous. In the house in Avondale they clustered around him in welcome. It was just like his ordination day all over again. The whole family was there, noisy in their pride of him: Mom, Pop, Rae, Nathan, Sam, little Hillel—some with spouses he had not yet met. He missed one face in the group. Brother Benjamin had died as a young man, during Nelson's first year abroad.

The good smell of Mom's cooking made time stand still, but when he looked at their faces Nelson realized how much his parents had aged while he was away. And Hillel was now Bar Mitzvah!

His mother, remembering how he loved fruit, had placed a filled bowl beside his chair, and they sat through hours of small talk, Nelson answering questions, telling them about Europe and Palestine. In their smiles and questions he lived it all over again—and knew he had indeed been gone a long time. How strange to sit in Cincinnati and describe Professor Albright—to make them see the dig at Tell Beit Mirsim—to picture for them how it felt to live in the Holy Land.

His mother's eyes did not leave him. How handsome he was, his dark hair and thick eyebrows framing those deep, expressive eyes, the mobile features tanned by the Palestinian sun.

Hadn't he been lonely, she wanted to know, over there so far away from them all?

Nelson smiled. Of course, he had missed them all. He had even missed their problems. But lonely? He had been far too busy. This past year especially, his head had been full. He had had to absorb all that pottery information. And next summer, when he went back, even more advanced studies awaited him.

What Anna really wanted to ask was, didn't he think it was time to get married? Several of her children were married now. They were already starting families. Nelson was such a good-looking man . . . he must have met someone he liked by this time. How long did he want to wait?

But she didn't ask those questions. One didn't ask them of a man like Nelson, not even if one was his mother. This was a Doctor of Philosophy, after all, who wasn't interested in an ordinary job or an ordinary wife. He didn't even as yet have a steady position. How then could he think of getting married?

Anna exhaled a secret sigh. It would take a very special girl to understand an unusual man like her son. She hoped Nelson would know when that right girl and the right time came along.

President Morgenstern at Hebrew Union College solved one of Nelson's problems. He, too, was happy to have his former student return to Cincinnati. He had kept up with Nelson's academic progress, and it pleased him to see how his encouragement had borne fruit. Such a promising young man would be an asset to the faculty of any good school. Since there was to be an opening for an instructor at the College the following season, would Nelson consent to fill it?

It was natural to be back at the school on Clifton Avenue, even if the roles were reversed. Now, instead of sitting in a classroom absorbing a lecture, it was he who stood before a brand-new generation of students, drumming facts into their heads. Nelson took his job seriously, drilling his charges endlessly, hammering verbs and grammar into them until the language became a part of their personality. The young men who had signed up for Hebrew in *his* class were going to *learn* Hebrew.

In later years his students might be grateful for his old-fashioned, determined instruction, but that would be much later. They smarted under his strict discipline, not knowing he was equally strict with himself. Only this past year in Palestine he had decided modern Arabic was necessary to his daily work. He had attended classes at a Syrian orphanage and not rested until his mastery of the language was secure.

Not all his students knew how to respond to him. One of them later recorded his impressions.

> During the first day of our Hebrew Grammar class, conducted by Dr. Nelson Glueck, Dr. Glueck called the roll. When he came across the names of Malcolm Stern and Dudley Weinberg, he stopped and asked, "What kind of names are these for Jewish boys who plan to become rabbis?"
>
> In those days we did not know Dr. Glueck very well, and when he spoke he was quite solemn. We just did not know whether to laugh or be quiet. He relieved the tension by telling us that when he was a student at the College, Dr. Neumark had asked the same question of him, and he had been waiting for an opportunity to do likewise.

Not even his students could misread the expression in Nelson's eyes when he spoke to them about the Holy Land. A virtual transformation came over him then. His

voice rose and fell when he described to them the hills and
wildernesses where divine purposes had been revealed.
His piercing dark eyes brimmed with tears when he
talked about the land whose soil had nurtured the world's
great religions. It was evident to his students then that the
man who stood before them was possessed by a great love.
Forgotten, for the moment, was the drillmaster who
insisted on precision in their grammatical declensions.

On a warm August evening in Jerusalem, Professor
Albright discussed Nelson's future plans with him. Despite the great heat, all the windows and doors at the
American School were shuttered and its staff was restricted by an early curfew to remain within the secure
walls of the building. Outside in the streets of the Old
City, several days of bloody Arab rioting had given way to
an uneasy silence.

"After three seasons with us, you will be ready for
something bigger the next time you come over, Nelson,"
Dr. Albright said.

Nelson agreed. At the end of this, his third summer in
Palestine, he suspected he had begun a pattern that
would be a permanent part of his life: winters of teaching
at the Hebrew Union College and summer months of sun,
sweat, and sand right here. As Professor Albright knew,
he was getting closer to his goal of doing his own
exploring.

"I've been thinking of the project you started some
years ago—investigating Transjordan," said Nelson. "If
the Arab-Jewish situation doesn't calm down during the
next year or two, it might be better if I work away from
this area."

"You still have Moab on your mind," smiled the
professor, "and I'm glad. That desert holds many a secret
we want to discover."

Albright had been one of the first to investigate
Transjordan—the other side of the Jordan. As early as
1924 he had found a number of sites he identified as
Moabite from the potsherds scattered about them. Although many another people had lived there, influencing
neighboring tribes through trade and ideas, little was
known about this territory in eastern Palestine. Its
ancient boundaries had never been mapped.

Albright encouraged Nelson in this project. So far the
area had been an archaeological stepchild; a survey of
Transjordan could be of vital importance. This would not
be an excavation but a surface exploration covering vast
desolate stretches of land that had so far hidden the
telltale clues of their former human habitation. Nelson
was hopeful that with natural logic and the descriptions in
his Bible he would find these clues. Of course there would
be risks. In this immense territory both nature and man
were hostile. The land was so bare of settlement—with
such a primitive level of human existence—that time had
apparently stood still there.

Fear did not deter Nelson. Somewhere in those
windswept empty deserts lay the legendary kingdoms of
the East. He would look for them.

Plans for such an ambitious project could not be made
overnight. Besides, another season of digging at Tell Beit
Mirsim lay ahead. Dr. Albright knew that Transjordan's
Department of Antiquities was interested in an exploration of the country; some of its experts might even wish to
join such an expedition. The professor promised to make
the necessary contacts. Certainly a summer's vacation
would not be long enough for this project. Did Nelson
think Hebrew Union College would grant him a leave of
absence?

As he packed his belongings by candlelight, preparing
for his departure the following day, Nelson did not feel as

depressed as he always did when leaving Jerusalem. This time the sadness of his farewell was tempered by the excitement of his forthcoming adventure. He smiled, thinking how calm life in Cincinnati would be this winter, compared to the tremendous experience awaiting him here in the near future.

Among the faculty of the Hebrew Union College several men felt pleasure in Nelson's rising success. The biblical scholars among them were, of course, interested in his work in the Holy Land. Some of them, like Dr. Morgenstern, had been his teachers and were proud of the progress he had made.

Adolph S. Oko, librarian at the College, was one of the men with a soft spot in his heart for Nelson. Though Nelson felt that the old man liked him, he was quite surprised when, one spring day in 1930, Mr. Oko ended a conversation on books by remarking, in his strong, uvular German accent, "I know a girrl you should meet. She's djust the sort of girrl you voud like."

Because he was handsome and was a good conversationalist, his company was eagerly sought. He received many invitations, but accepted few. His life was far too filled with important plans to allow for social games involving young ladies. Nelson was flattered that Mr. Oko should go to the trouble of introducing him to a girl, but he did not take the offer too seriously.

He did not know that Mr. Oko had already put in a telephone call to Helen, the daughter of his good friend Dr. Sam Iglauer, in which he said: "I vant you to meet a man. He's the handsomest man I've ever seen. But that's not all."

Seldom had bright, dark-eyed Helen Iglauer received such an intriguing description of a young man. She agreed to be introduced to Nelson Glueck. On a June evening in

1930 Helen returned to her home in Cincinnati's Clifton section and said to her mother: "Today I met the most handsome man I've ever seen."

Mrs. Iglauer found this announcement a bit startling. Her daughter, a sophomore at the University of Cincinnati Medical School, had never uttered such a romantic statement before, and she knew many young men. Only a few days passed before Mrs. Iglauer could verify her daughter's impression. The young man in question asked to call on Helen at her home.

The Iglauers were prominent members of Cincinnati's German-Jewish community. Helen's paternal grandfather had come to America during the 1860s, when a wave of German immigrants left their homeland because they found the political injustice there intolerable. Her maternal grandfather, Joseph Ransohoff, was born in America, studied in Europe, and became the founder of the department of surgery in the College of Medicine of the University of Cincinnati. Her father, Dr. Samuel Iglauer, specialized in plastic surgery, bronchoscopy, and was a pioneer in disorders of the ear, nose, and throat. In his specialty he was chairman of the department for over twenty years. When Dr. Sam Iglauer married Helen Ransohoff, he cemented two medical families together. The young couple raised Helen, her sister, and her brother in an old Victorian stone house in a tree-shaded garden not far from the university and the medical school.

Almost from the first Nelson became fond of the house at 162 Glenmary Avenue. The comfortable three-story home gave him pleasure. The lofty ceilings, the tall windows overlooking the well-cared-for garden, the solid cherry wood furniture were a big change from the crowded quarters in which he had grown up. He decided quickly that he liked the Iglauers, their gracious style of living, their hospitality—and their daughter.

Helen was different from most girls he had known. An attractive girl, she could easily have picked a suitable husband from among the young men in her family's large circle of friends. Marriage was not Helen's final goal. She chose a profession despite the objections of her surgeon father, who knew the obstacles that women in medicine faced every day.

Helen was a girl who knew what she wanted—and went after it. Her career was important to her. However, when she met Nelson Glueck she decided that he, too, would be important in her life—perhaps even more important than her career.

As usual Nelson's summer plans were made, and the moment college sessions were over he sailed for Palestine. This time, in the heat and sand of Tell Beit Mirsim, it occurred to Nelson that the careful schedule he had constructed for himself for the next few years might have to be bent a little to accommodate the pretty, young medical student whom he could not get out of his mind.

That fall Nelson, in his most persuasive manner, proposed marriage to Helen. The locale for the proposal was Nelson's favorite spot in the Iglauer house—the large living room. Dr. Iglauer's custom of reading the evening paper had terminated as usual: he had fallen asleep behind it on the deeply cushioned sofa. In one corner of the room the two young people carried on a quiet conversation. In the midst of it Dr. Iglauer awoke to a more heated discussion.

"But you *are* a rabbi," he heard his daughter say, "and if I marry you, that'll make me a rebbetzin. Well, that's just not for me."

At that point Dr. Iglauer decided to stay behind his newspaper and pretend he was still sleeping. His arms were quite stiff, but the embarrassment of the moment was worse, so he persisted.

"Of course, I'm a rabbi," Nelson was replying, "but I'm not a practicing one. I decided that long ago. Even that would be no obstacle, if you felt about me the way you should."

Helen mentioned other barriers to their marriage. She wanted a medical career, which would tie her down to Cincinnati. How about his frequent absences on those expeditions where she could not accompany him?

Suddenly the proposal turned into a hot quarrel. Seeing his best salesmanship getting nowhere, Nelson's mercurial temperament rose to the surface. He left the Iglauer home in a hurry, his mission frustrated.

Hearing the front door slam, Dr. Iglauer decided it was safe to come out from behind his newspaper.

"You'd better say yes," he advised his now speechless daughter. "That's quite a young man you've got there. I'd marry him if I were you."

Helen's opposition only increased Nelson's determination. He admired bright women, and he knew he would never be bored with Helen. She, like him, was far too interested in the world to allow life to become dull. They might have an unusual marriage, but it would be a good one.

Of course Helen wanted to marry Nelson. She knew of no other young man nearly as appealing to her as he. The dashing, handsome archaeologist would be a perfect match to her own career. Nelson's brilliance and vigor would take him far, and she wanted to be there with him.

On a blustery March Sunday in 1931 Helen and Nelson were married. Receiving the congratulations of their wedding guests, Helen smiled wistfully at the tall, handsome bridegroom standing next to her. Only she knew they would not be together long. Barely six weeks from now Nelson would be off again—digging at Tell Beit Mirsim with Dr. Albright.

6

ON AN EARLY MORNING in December 1932, while only a few inhabitants looked on in sleepy amazement, Nelson Glueck led a caravan of seven people on horseback through the town of Mafraq in northern Transjordan, headed eastward for the desert.

Life in Mafraq was quiet. One of the few interesting pastimes the customers of the local Arab coffeehouse had was to speculate on the infrequent visitors to their town. It was clear that the troop of seven they were watching this December day must have important reasons for traveling through Mafraq.

The caravan's tall, slender leader was everywhere, gesturing, arranging, directing. The pack horses bearing food, bedding, and scientific equipment meant little to the coffeehouse observers. Perhaps these foreigners were interested in putting in oil pipelines or discovering precious metals. But the townspeople noted with special attention the truck carrying six armed soldiers and an officer of the Arab Legion which followed the little company at a slow speed, obviously detailed to guard it against the dangers of the desert.

Nelson rode out at the head of the group. By his side was his young bride, Helen. Nelson, sunburned and wearing an Arab headdress, was now the acting director of the American School of Oriental Research, and this was his first extensive exploration of Transjordan. Along on

48

the expedition were several specialists working for the Transjordan Department of Antiquities.

Besides Helen Glueck, one other woman accompanied the men. She was Mrs. George Horsefield, wife of the director of the Transjordan Department of Antiquities. The group had its complement of mapmakers, photographers, pottery experts, and draftsmen.

Mafraq had been chosen as the starting point because of its convenient location near the abandoned tracks of the Transjordan Railway. These tracks ran parallel to the boundaries of Transjordan and would serve as a guide. Toward the west nothing but wasteland spread before the eyes of the travelers, but on the eastern side of the railroad fertile hilly territory greeted their gaze. Here a chain of hills divided the land between the desert and tilled soil. It was on these peaks that Nelson hoped he might find remnants of the ancient Edomite and Moabite fortresses that had once formed the eastern frontier of these two biblical kingdoms.

His target point for the whole exploration was Kilwa, a crossroads at the southern end of Transjordan, near the Arabian border. Between Mafraq and Kilwa lay the whole vast desert country in which Nelson hoped to locate and list as many settlements of historical value as he could.

In this dusty, dry part of the world, water is of prime importance. Without it, no one could live and raise food. From the start, the members of the expedition knew that the first thing they must look for was water. A nearby spring or stream, or the remains of a cistern, would be certain clues that the area had once been inhabited. When they did find obvious signs of water, there were usually potsherds too. But there were other clues to be found in the topography of these biblical lands, and Nelson soon learned how to decipher them. He learned that throughout Transjordan roads and highways had always followed the mountainous backbone of the country. A natural border was formed where the mountains ended and the desert began. And it was here—at this borderline—that most of the country's stream beds were found.

Once in a while such a stream bed—called a *wadi* in Arabic—might be completely dried out. Most of them did yield groundwater with very little digging, however, and Bedouins traveling the desert with their flocks made use of the stream beds to provide water for their goats, camels, and horses.

Each time he observed this phenomenon, Nelson thought of the biblical quotation describing it poetically: "Thus saith the Lord, 'I will make this torrent-bed nothing but cisterns. You will see neither wind nor rain, yet the torrent-bed shall be filled with water.' "

Nelson knew that the desert held the ruins of several castles, so he was not surprised when, shortly after leaving Mafraq, the expedition found the remains of an elaborate structure. Close by was an empty water reservoir and several large, inactive cisterns.

On their way into the heart of the desert the group found several more castles, each with its own system of water storage. These ruins were definitely not prehistoric but, Nelson judged, belonged to the period of early Arab princedoms. Both he and his colleagues were impressed by the extraordinary skill in the use of water engineering displayed by these systems, which had been built to catch excess rain during the wet winter seasons for storage against the long dry spells. Now this part of the desert was completely uninhabited and desolate.

One morning during this exploration, members of the Glueck expedition rode into a small village located on a hilltop. In the fashion of the desert they asked for water for their horses, but they were told that there was no water in the village. Nelson found this hard to believe. He had seen several cisterns on his way up to the village. He asked for the village chieftain, repeated his request, and was told the same thing.

All water was brought from a spring quite a distance away. Every day the village women took their jugs to the spring outside the town, filled them with water, and walked home again. On this day they had not yet returned, as the visitor could tell for himself.

Looking in the direction pointed out by the elder, Nelson saw the village women approach the mountain, carrying their water jugs on their heads. On their way home they passed right by the unused cisterns.

It seemed incredible that no one had thought of cleaning and repaving the ancient cisterns. To Nelson it was so obvious that much of this wasteland could be made productive and capable of sustaining life with just some repair work.

Just as important as the finding of water was the locating of ancient roads and highways. Desert Bedouins still traveled trails that had been in use by their ancestors long ago. Other roads, once major caravan routes, had been enlarged and paved by the Romans to accommodate their military might.

All such roads must have been ideal sites for trading posts and fortified towns, and once the archaeologists discovered the main lines of the highways they usually charted many settlements here. Many times they found unexpectedly interesting stories at the same time.

Of particular fascination to Nelson was a main central highway through Transjordan which he saw for the first time when he flew over the territory by plane. Nelson discovered that the highway was called the "Sultan's Road" in modern Arabic, but he also found it to be identical with parts of the famous Trajan's Road, built by the Romans during the second century C.E.

As Nelson described it:

Centuries and millennia before, the same line of roadway was already in use, because of practically the same geographical, topographical and economic reasons. When the messengers of Moses came from Qadesh-Barnea to the kings of Edom and Moab, they promised them that the Israelites would hew to the line of the "King's Highway," the royal road, turning neither to the right nor to the left of it, and paying for whatsoever they obtained in food and drink. What is this "King's Highway" which cut through central Transjordan as early as the time of Moses? Where did this "royal" road lead to? . . . It is nothing more and nothing less than the very same highway, or the line of that highway which in due course of time became Trajan's Road and which today has become Emir Abdullah's Road. The King's Highway led from Aqabah to Syria.

From his knowledge of the Bible, and the information he gathered during the desert survey, Nelson produced his own footnote to the history of the Exodus.

It must have been springtime when the Israelites, refused permission to travel through Edom and Moab, were compelled to go eastward around these countries and find their way through the desert. Only at this season of the year could man and beast in large numbers have found sufficient water and grazing to survive the rigors of the way.

Nelson and the members of his party returned safely to Jerusalem. There he and Helen settled into their apartment at the American School for the length of the leave granted him by Hebrew Union College.

With the help of Dr. Albright and others from the American School, Nelson went over photographs and materials from this first leg of the Transjordan survey and found the trip had been quite worthwhile.

Many more exploratory excursions would have to be made, and Nelson planned three more short trips into Transjordan for the spring of 1933. He was looking forward to the new year, when he would be able to delve deeply into the past of the desert. He loved the work he was doing, and his efforts were already recognized as major contributions to biblical archaeology.

Impatient for spring to come, neither Nelson nor anyone else could fathom that in the heart of Europe a new, catastrophic episode in the story of the Jewish people would have its birth during that same spring of 1933.

The blazing eastern sun of Transjordan burned down over the endless miles of desert. To Nelson it seemed as if he were alone in the world, alone except for the presence of Ali Abu Ghosh, his Arab companion, and the camel boy who pulled the pack animal laden with their camping equipment. But he knew he was not alone. His presence in the desert had been observed and through some mysterious tribal grapevine had been broadcast to unseen inhabitants of these waste lands.

But Nelson, by now experienced in the etiquette of the desert, knew what was expected of him. Before entering this region he had inquired about the local chieftain who reigned over the territory. He had asked the way to the campsite of this sheik and was even now on his way to it.

After several hours of riding, Ali Abu Ghosh suddenly raised his arm in signal. Ahead of them, like a mirage, appeared the faint outlines of an encampment. As if in affirmation that the travelers had been seen, several horsemen in white robes were approaching them.

When the riders were close enough, Nelson stopped them with a shout. In Arabic he explained that he wanted to meet their chief and pay his respects. He had not failed to notice that the men were heavily armed. He was counting on the traditional hospitality of the Arab, however, and it seemed he was not to be disappointed.

One man led the way, two others rode on either side of Nelson and his companion. The camel boy followed.

When they reached the camp Nelson was taken to the guest tent. There, amid much politeness, he greeted— and in return was greeted by—the man seated in the midst of a group of men gathered around a burning brazier. Each man held a tiny cup filled with bitter, black coffee flavored with cardamon seeds. These cups were constantly refilled from the large pot bubbling on the coals of the brazier.

Nelson found his hosts extremely friendly. They moved over to allow him room to sit next to them, spreading blankets for his comfort while seated on the ground. To make it easier for him to recline, one man brought a camel saddle against which Nelson could lean. Soon one of the tiny coffee cups was put into his hands, and he was surprised to find how the hot, strong brew almost immediately relieved his weariness.

Nelson watched with interest as one man prepared to serve tea to the group. When the small water kettle, half-filled with sugar, came to a boil, a handful of tea leaves was added to it. After the mixture boiled once more, the chieftain brought out a special portable case holding small glasses. He rinsed each glass carefully, then filled it with tea and presented it to one of his guests. Again Nelson was astonished to find how refreshing this hot, sweet mixture was to a tired desert traveler.

Between sipping the liquids all the men conversed with

him. From previous visits to the guest tents of tribal chiefs, Nelson had discovered that conversation was a major pleasure among the Arabs. They loved to talk and did it in lengthy fashion. Although Nelson would have preferred to get to the point of his visit as quickly as possible, he knew that sooner or later he would accomplish this despite the lengthy formalities of tribal protocol. If he wanted to accomplish something in this tent, he must bide his time. And so Nelson laughed and joked with the best of them, telling his own stories in Arabic that brought roars from the gathered Bedouins.

Soon it was feast time. No self-respecting sheik would entertain a guest without providing a generous meal for him. Once again Nelson found that feasting in an Arab tent was a strenuous task.

Enormous dishes of steaming mutton and goat meat, floating atop a huge mountain of rice, were placed at the feet of the diners. Everyone, except the host, partook of the repast. Nelson watched as the men around him rolled up their sleeves, reached into the bowl, and grabbed a handful of rice.

Soon he followed their example and opened his mouth to receive the ball of rice and the chunk of meat he sent after it. Out of the corner of his eye he saw the chieftain take his jeweled silver dagger and cut up an especially choice section of the meat, which he tossed in Nelson's direction. Nodding his appreciation, Nelson put the tidbit into his mouth, as he was expected to do. In Arab fashion he used only the fingers of his right hand in eating. With his left hand he held a cup of sour goat's milk with which he washed down the food.

The elaborate and ceremonious courtesies within the guest tent were not without drawbacks. Urged to eat food alien and unnatural to his taste, Nelson often suffered gastric discomfort. The vermin-laden blankets his hosts pushed on him for warmth during the chill desert nights resulted in untold flea bites. But both were necessary to gain good will.

For sooner or later the conversation came around to the visitor's purpose in being in these parts. And then came the time for Nelson to explain that he was interested in the history of the region, that he had come to study it and the people who had once lived here—long before the lifetime of the present occupants. He wished to explore the sheik's territory.

He never failed to receive the chieftain's gracious permission to study the land as much as he wished. Under the protection of his host, accompanied perhaps by one or more of his tribesmen, Nelson was free to roam the area. His guards not only showed him the sites he wanted to see, they also protected him from hostile neighboring tribes.

Nelson learned his lesson in desert etiquette early. He practiced it throughout his many years of exploring the wilderness. He never experienced true fear even when, alone except for Ali Abu Ghosh, he ranged through the whole Transjordan countryside. He knew that he could feel safe wherever he put down his sleeping bag in the lonely sands of the desert. As a guest of the local sheik he was protected and free from harm.

On camelback, clad in Bedouin robes and accompanied by his Arab companion, Nelson certainly did not look the picture of a rabbi. It was just as well that he did not. The Transjordan desert presented enough dangers to an ordinary traveler, both from nature and from local residents. The Arabs, rehearsing for their future holy wars on the Jews of Palestine, would never have welcomed him so warmly had they known his real background.

Nelson was fully aware that his daring had its risks. He

admitted himself that it was so unheard of for a Jew to wander alone through Transjordan that no one thought to ask his religion.

But there were times when even Nelson's self-discipline and willpower were not enough to keep him from danger. Once Nelson, his colleague Reginald Head, and Ali Abu Ghosh wandered near the Red Sea on foot and were overcome by the burning heat. Their drinking water gone, their lips blistered and cracked by the sun, the trio's exhaustion became acute.

> After a while it became possible to make progress only by resting for fifteen minutes after walking ten. . . . At about five o'clock Ali collapsed. I shall not soon forget how he looked, as, lying on the ground, he gasped to me: "If you don't bring me some water, I shall die." I loosened his collar and wiped his lips clean of dried foam. Head and I struggled on. Finally I was done in and simply could not continue. Suddenly it just didn't matter anymore. The earth seemed to rise to meet me, and I hugged it. . . . Head, good old Head, carried on until, after what seemed to be ages later, he stumbled on a small spring and dropped exhausted. There, several Arabs found him, and then came for us . . .

Despite the heat, the flies, and the fine sand that constantly invaded his food and his clothing, Nelson enjoyed the desert. The vast emptiness was healing balm to him, and far from vacant.

> I have never yet looked east toward the hills of Moab without being seized by a sense of excitement. I have never yet started climbing steeply

toward their tops without wondering what new mystery would reveal itself to me. For these lands, east as well as west of the Jordan, are haunted by the shades of history and throb with the pulse of the past. These are more than conglomerations of rock and soil, with springs and plants, animals and people. These are the haunts of the children of God, and His Spirit is imprinted in the very atmosphere. I have stood on the shores of the Red Sea and heard the accents of Jehova in Sinai. I have wandered in the wastes of the desert and heard the weeping of Hagar. I have sat in the tents of Ishmael and found myself peering into the faces of the prophets. I have paced along the banks of the Jordan and watched the people of Israel crossing over to the Land of Promise.

When one slept under the open sky every night, life was simple. Tea, rice, dried fruit, Arab bread—man needed so little to sustain his body. It was amazing how much easier it became to understand the Bible when one read it in the lands of its origin. Every direction fell into place here. Every Old Testament description told him what the potsherds were later to confirm. For Nelson, the scholar-scientist with the soul of a poet, the desert was the place where the past came alive.

From 1932 until 1946, when he finally reached Kilwa, Nelson returned to the Transjordan desert summer after summer, exploring the whole territory systematically. Sometimes he came alone, sometimes Ali Abu Ghosh accompanied him. At other times he led expeditions sponsored by the various schools with which he was associated.

His findings, published under the title "Explorations in

Eastern Palestine" in the *Bulletin of the American School of Oriental Research,* were to change the thinking of archaeologists working in the Holy Land.

During these arduous journeys Nelson charted over one thousand previously unknown settlements by identifying the pottery remains he found near the sites. This alone proved that the Transjordan desert was never the wilderness it had been believed to be. Though it had been uninhabited for very long stretches of time, the desert had been occupied during several periods of its history and had supported human and animal life with its water holes and stretches of grazing lands.

One of Nelson's earliest objectives was also fulfilled by these years of surveying Transjordan.

> Figurines, inscriptions, steles, pottery fragments, sacred objects and the ancient sites on which they occur (many of which throughout the length of Transjordan are connected by the "King's Highway"), and also mines and metals,—these are the materials of history gained by gleaning from the surface ruins still left in Edom, Moab, Ammon and Gilead. They testify to the reality and to the kind of kingdoms which once existed on the Other Side of the Jordan, alongside the kingdoms of Israel and Judah.

One of the theories brought to light by Nelson's explorations along the shores of the Dead Sea was that the Exodus of the Israelites could not have taken place when historians thought it had. Egyptian inscriptions, royal records, and local traditions had led scholars to believe that the wandering of the Israelites from Egypt to Canaan had occurred during the fifteenth century B.C.E. Nelson thought this incorrect.

Aided by biblical clues and his pottery dating, Nelson reasoned that both Edom and Moab were strongly organized, fortified kingdoms during the thirteenth century B.C.E. This was the only time in history when these two kingdoms were strong enough to have repelled the wandering Israelites. It was then that they refused the Israelites permission to pass through their countries. Accordingly, Nelson placed the date of the Exodus around 1300 B.C.E., and modern scholars have accepted his dating as definitive.

7

SITTING ON THE GROUND in the desert south of the Dead Sea one evening in the spring of 1934, Nelson found he had a puzzle on his hands. On his lap lay his Bible, open to the passage in chapter 8 of Deuteronomy in which Moses described the Promised Land to his wandering people. One particular verse of the passage had interested Nelson for a long time. It was, in fact, the reason for his being here right now.

The fascinating verse talked about a place "whose stones are iron, and out of whose hills thou mayest dig brass." And Nelson asked himself, was this poetry or literal truth? How accurate was the Bible in the description of physical details? Did he have any justification for believing that such a place really existed?

Nelson had read geological reports which told of mineral deposits in the area where he was now, the territory of the Wadi Arabah. The geological reports even mentioned copper. Could this be the "brass" the Bible spoke of? Where in this windswept, waterless desert would he find such a rich treasure of ore?

This time Nelson was not alone. He was accompanied by a member of his own American School and by a friend working for the Transjordan Department of Antiquities. A faculty member from Hebrew Union College in Cincinnati, too, had joined the group. Some of the men had visited this area before and were familiar with the same geological reports Nelson had read. They were as interested as Nelson in finding out more about the scientifically mysterious past of the Wadi Arabah.

Sitting close to Nelson in the fading light of the evening was his faithful guide, Sheik Audeh ibn Ahmed el-Asfar, who, with five members of his tribe and nine camels, was accompanying the American expedition through the Wadi Arabah. The timeless landscape, his pleasantly smiling companion who baked unleavened bread for their evening meal, which they ate in the softly swirling mists of the desert, made it all too easy for Nelson's fertile imagination to believe he was living in the days of the Exodus. Transporting himself back to the time of the Israelites and their wandering was simple: he had only to look at the cragged hills in the distance and at the face of the helpful sheik, and he imagined himself a part of that people on the move, guided through these treacherous desert mountains by a local chieftain who knew his terrain well.

Nelson had been talking to the guide about possible sites that might have once been used for mining, and Sheik Audeh suggested a nearby large ruin that might interest the professor. To the local Bedouins the site was known as the Khirbet Nahas (Arabic for the "copper ruin").

"Why is it called that?" Nelson asked.

The sheik shrugged his shoulders, smiling. He did not know.

Did the other men of the tribe know why the ruin had its name? Nelson glanced in the direction of the tribesmen grouped near their grazing camels.

None of them did, the guide explained.

How, then, did the sheik know about this ruin?

Oh, everyone in the area knew about the Khirbet Nahas. Their fathers had already known about it.

Did anyone recall copper being mined there?

The ruin was old, much too old to be a working mine. It had not been used in a long, long time.

Nelson saw it was useless to question the sheik any further. Obviously at home here in the Wadi Arabah, the guides knew all about the location of trails that would get the expedition to its desired sites. But the tribesmen had not been trained to look for the same information as the scientists who had come here to search. Their business was guiding. It was up to the archaeologists to find and evaluate the clues this area held secret.

The Wadi Arabah, which cuts through Palestine, dividing east from west, is a large desert depression that extends from the Dead Sea southward to the Gulf of Aqabah. It is part of a huge fracture in the crust of the earth which runs from the Taurus Mountains in Asia Minor to beyond the Red Sea in Africa. Geologists surmise that a gigantic earthquake took place in the Jordan Valley, one of the many earthquakes characteristic of the region. Such an episode has been recorded in the Bible's memory: the stories about Sodom and Gomorrah describe in graphic detail the "fire and brimstone" that accompanied an earthquake. The bleak, uninhabited landscape of the Wadi Arabah is one result of such an unequaled disaster. Volcanic lava and black basalt rocks remain as witnesses to the upheavals which often took place here.

From his intimate knowledge of the Bible, Nelson knew that this wasteland of the Wadi Arabah, despite its forbidding appearance, had always been supremely important to the history of Israel. For centuries violent warfare had raged between the peoples seeking control of this region. What was so important about the land that kings would risk armies in a life-and-death struggle here? Why had Judaeans fought Edomites over this piece of inhospitable territory, exhausting themselves so in their constant warring that they became easy prey to foreign invaders, who finally conquered them both?

Of course, the Wadi Arabah had always been an essential caravan route between Palestine and Transjordan, leading also to Egypt and Arabia. But there were other reasons why it had been fought over so much. Could it be that the biblical verse he found so intriguing also contained the clue to this question? Nelson felt he was about to stumble onto something important. He was too good a scientist to rely on instinct alone, but science, he was certain, would help him to substantiate his hunch. Wrapping himself in his Bedouin cloak, Nelson followed the example of his guide and stretched out on the sand for the night.

Early the following morning the guides led Nelson and his companions to the site of the "copper ruin." The Americans took a close look at the curiously colored blue and green veins in the sandstone hills that surrounded the ruin in a semi-circle. They chipped off samples of rock for further testing before they admitted that they had indeed found copper.

Nelson walked around the area and surveyed it from every direction. What he found amazed even him. He discovered great heaps of copper slag near a number of small wrecked smelting furnaces. He saw ruins of once-large buildings. Alongside them he found huge amounts of raw, unused sandstone. Farther away he saw tremendous piles of crumbled masonry that must have once been a large walled enclosure, surrounding an area of small huts, a few of which still stood intact. At one side of the enclosure lay the destroyed remains of guard towers, suggesting that the site had been well fortified.

Fortifications here, in this barren terrain so isolated from other human habitations? A closer look at the poor, bare living quarters and Nelson surmised that the place had once been a prison camp. The huts had served as shelter for the miners, probably slaves or prisoners of war, who had been forced to work here under duress.

If a large group of men had existed in these bare hills, how had they lived? There were no water holes here, no visible means of raising food. Even the wood to stoke the smelting furnaces did not grow nearby. And what of the ore mined and smelted here—where had it been taken for refining and further working?

Above all, in a land so metal-poor, who had benefited from the exploitation of this area, which seemed rich beyond belief?

For Nelson the answer to the last question was provided by the numerous potsherds he found near the surface of Khirbet Nahas. Eroded by time and fine sand, some fragments were still complete enough to tell their story. They had been a part of the pottery used in the daily lives of the miners who worked here. It was crude ware he was looking at—jugs and containers used for water, grain, and other foodstuffs. But it was all of the same period: Iron Age pottery.

When he compared notes with others in the expedition, men who also knew the pottery code, it confirmed to him that he was right to date the shards as he had done. This pottery was made during the lifetime of the great King Solomon. It must be presumed that the mining camp had been operated during the reign of the same ruler!

Traveling farther, the expedition found that Khirbet Nahas was not only the largest mining camp in the area, but apparently the center of a whole chain of other such operations. Hidden within the hills of the winding wadis were many other mining sites—so many, in fact, that at a later time, when Nelson flew over the area, he could see other, new, sites from the air but could not pinpoint the ones he had visited on the ground. He theorized that all were part of one organized system of mining and distribution, Later, more extensive exploration added to his theory that the mining operation was the basis of King Solomon's commercial enterprises.

As they moved through the Wadi Arabah, finding one mining site after another, the members of the American expedition found more clues to complete their profile of the merchant king, Solomon, under whose rule the Israelites and Judaeans were united into one great realm. It became clear that the mining operation could have come about only through well-planned organization and supervision. It must have been a man of wide vision, aided by capable advisors, who planned it.

How had the problem of fuel been handled, for instance? No trees grew in the Arabah. The shrubs and bushes struggling in the desert would have never sufficed to heat the cauldrons of bubbling ore. How had the miners melted down their precious product? The Glueck expedition concluded that the dense forests of Edom must have supplied the fuel. There, in an area where trees grew in heavy stands, wood was cut down and burned into charcoal. In that form the fuel became more easily transportable.

In an area so utterly dry as the Wadi Arabah, mining was possible only during winter and early spring, when the scant rains could be caught in large storage jars. Even that was not sufficient at times. Had large caravan trains of donkeys wound their way up the desolate mountain trails, bringing in food, water, and the charcoal fuel to the miners and their guards? And had the merchants in the caravans exchanged their goods in these hills for the smelted copper, which was carried out of the Wadi Arabah to the place or places where it could be refined?

The Glueck expedition traveled the whole length of the Wadi Arabah. At different hours of the day, in varying shades of sunlight, they found colors in the rocks which indicated mineral deposits. At each stop the men tested rock samples. Almost always they found copper and iron ore, but also malachite, a green mineral native to the region.

Every time their tests for copper and iron ore came up positive, the men checked the territory a little more carefully. They were almost certain they would find openings and pillars cut into the sandstone hills— galleries dug into the rock, proving that ancient mines had been worked here once.

Nelson's mind was still filled with speculation. Where had the precious ore from those crucibles traveled to? Where was the great refining center where the metal had been smelted and shaped into the ingots traded by the great King Solomon for the rare treasures listed in the Bible, "the gold, and silver, ivory, and apes, and peacocks"?

So much of the puzzle already fitted. But now time had run out again. The expedition had to disband, its members to return another time. Already Nelson was turning over another biblical quotation which gave him no peace. He was convinced that it provided further proof he was on the right trail.

Somewhere King Solomon had a seaport from which he traded with all the known countries of his day. "And King Solomon made a navy of ships in Ezion-geber, which is beside Eloth, on the shore of the Red Sea, in the land of Edom." This was the clue from which he must work—the next time.

A sad day begins like any other day, with an opened shade and a cup of coffee—and, in Nelson's case, there was also a morning class in Bible history to teach. The news that Papa had taken a turn for the worse came later. For days things had stood badly for Morris Glueck, but the family was optimistic. The strength and courage that had always seen him through would not desert him now. It was unthinkable that the Gluecks would have to do without Papa, the head of the clan, the rock who had always held them together.

In the afternoon a telephone call to Hebrew Union College informed Professor Glueck that he had better come—his father had gone into a coma. Jake Marcus was nearby when the call came. Without a word he put on his overcoat and walked out with Nelson. The news affected him as well. Knowing the Gluecks through these many years, they were his family too.

A taxi ride brought them to the Glueck house in Avondale and a big family gathering. Nelson walked into his parents' bedroom. He touched his mother on the shoulder as she sat beside the bed. He knew there was nothing else for him to do here now.

Jake Marcus recalls that he and Nelson walked for hours. There was silence between the friends that April afternoon. Both knew that they were holding a death watch. In the Glueck house all the brothers and sisters were sitting in the grief-filled living room, quietly wrapped in their own thoughts. Nelson and his friend walked off their sorrow.

Papa had shared Nelson's discoveries of the Solomonic copper mines the previous year. Nelson could not tell him enough; Papa was intensely interested in his son's descriptions. It was miraculous that Nelson had been privileged to find the very trails over which the children of Israel had walked in their Exodus from Egypt. It was fantastic that his own son should be the one to discover the foundations of King Solomon's wealth.

Morris had looked up at the tall, heavy-browed man, his own son. He remembered their Sunday excursions to the Indian mounds and smiled when he thought about the little boy who had constantly asked questions.

"I should have answered more of your questions, son," he said with a half-serious face, "but I guess I did the best I could."

And Nelson had shared with him their own private joke. He knew that Morris had always done his best for him and that now Papa was enormously pleased at the way things had turned out for his son.

It was a good feeling, too, for Nelson to show off his accomplishments to Papa. Success is sweeter when a loved one shares it. He was already a famous man in the academic world, but Nelson always found a great satisfaction being right here in the living room with his father.

He talked about some of these things with Jake on their lengthy walk. Jake understood him. He knew how important it had always been to Nelson to please his father. And Jake assured him that he had fulfilled all of Morris's expectations.

The two men returned to the house and found it filled with sounds of soft sobbing. It was all over. Morris's heart had stopped beating. Once more Nelson stepped into the bedroom. He bent over his father and kissed his forehead in a long and loving final kiss.

When he came out of the room, Nelson's face was inscrutable. His great sadness was hidden under a veil, distant and remote. Quietly he put on his overcoat against the chill of the April afternoon. Then he and Jake Marcus left, heading for the house on Glenmary where Helen was waiting.

It was 1938 before Nelson resumed his search for King Solomon's mysterious seaport. In the meantime he had become a full professor of the Bible and biblical archaeology at Hebrew Union College, and as director of the American School of Oriental Research he pursued his survey of the vast stretches of Transjordan. He had become important enough for top American scientific organizations to be interested in his work. Recognizing the value of his research in the Wadi Arabah, both the Smithsonian Institution and the American Philosophical Society granted him funds for the continuation of his project.

With these funds Nelson equipped a full expedition. This time he would do more than survey the territory. His first camel train left Jerusalem in March 1938, bearing a large team of geologists, historians, excavators, a photographer, and much equipment.

The caravan followed Nelson's earlier southward trek and traveled the full length of the Wadi Arabah, until it reached the Gulf of Aqabah. Nelson had a definite goal this time. It was a small mound located near the head of the gulf, a site known as Tell el-Kheleifeh. During his 1934 survey Nelson had visited this site, not knowing that just before him a German archaeologist by the name of Fritz Frank had been digging in the area. Fritz Frank discovered Tell el-Kheleifeh. He found that the mound contained many pottery shards, which he judged to be very ancient. Frank, too, was looking for King Solomon's seaport, Ezion-geber, and he believed that Tell el-Kheleifeh was it. Not being able to use the pottery code, Frank could not prove he had found Ezion-geber.

Unaware during his first trip of the importance the German explorer attributed to the site, Nelson had examined the pieces of pottery he found scattered so lavishly around the ruin. To his excited amazement, the potsherds matched the ones he had found earlier in the mining camps. Just as he had dated the pieces found at the

Khirbet Nahas as belonging to the Iron Age, Nelson now confirmed that the pottery of Tell el-Kheleifeh belonged to the same period. It was a spectacular discovery. Over and over, during the next few years, Nelson was to ask himself: if that pottery was made during and after the lifetime of King Solomon, had he found the missing piece in the puzzle?

Like all accomplished men, Nelson knew that every discovery he made was only a link in the chain which binds one generation of scholars to the next. Each man is bound to the ideas of the man before him, which he can either improve or reject. Just as his own teacher, Professor Albright, had moved in the footsteps of an earlier archaeologist, Flinders Petrie, in perfecting the pottery identification code, so Nelson now found himself bringing the assumption of Fritz Frank closer to reality, giving credit to the earlier archaeologist for the discovery at Tell el-Kheleifeh.

It was Tell el-Kheleifeh that now drew Nelson. Impatient for the journey through the austere, solitary Wadi Arabah to end, his eyes scanned the horizon until finally the town of Aqabah, glittering white in the dazzling sun, came into view.

> I shall never forget the day we came to the crest of the inconspicuous watershed near the southern end of the Wadi Arabah, and saw the deep blue tongue of the Gulf of Aqabah ahead of us. It extended southward as far as one could see between haze-shrouded hills of forbidding mien, forming a jagged barrier on either side. Our camels, sniffing the moisture in the air and anticipating the sweet water they must have sensed awaited them, quickened their pace and soon broke into a steady run. Our weariness suddenly

vanished. At this junction of the continents of Asia and Africa, the boundaries of Arabia, Transjordan, Palestine and Sinai touch the northern end of the gulf, with parts of all of them becoming visible to us. This was the scene that had presented itself to the people of the Exodus. We were racing forward into the past. And soon we reached the water's edge, near which Ezion-geber had once stood.

But when the caravan reached the busy seaport of Aqabah, Nelson ordered his camel drivers to go beyond the town, making straight for the small mound sitting amid the sand dunes of the desert about 500 yards from the actual shore line. This was Tell el-Kheleifeh.

Had the men of the expedition not known Nelson's reasoning, they might have wondered why their leader had chosen the most uncomfortable spot in the whole area for setting up their tents. Their encampment lay in the direct path of every windy draft that blew out of the Wadi Arabah. They tasted sand with every mouthful of nourishment. Grit rubbed their skin raw. Even fresh water was unavailable here—it had to be sent in from Aqabah four miles to the east.

But long before the caravan reached Tell el-Kheleifeh, Professor Glueck had explained to his co-workers the results of his previous visit to the mound. He had told them why he felt this particular spot was important enough for a full-scale excavation.

As they all knew, Nelson Glueck was a surface man. With the exception of his apprenticeship at Tell Beit Mirsim with Dr. Albright and the excavation of a temple in Transjordan, almost all of his work had been in land surveys. On his stops along the Wadi Arabah—the "Valley of the Desert"—he had learned enough from visiting the sites and studying the potsherds how to date and identify his material. All this changed now that they were at Tell el-Kheleifeh.

It seemed such an unimpressive rubble heap, hardly worth investigating. Even Nelson was almost tempted to look around for another site which would look more like the ruins of King Solomon's great seaport ought to look. But there was no other tell in the area. And Nelson knew those potsherds would not lie.

He had come to the last step in solving his puzzle—right here on the site where they had erected the camp. Early tomorrow morning they would begin digging their first test shaft. A most exciting venture was about to start.

8

"And king solomon made a navy of ships in Eziongeber, which is beside Eloth, on the shore of the Red Sea, in the land of Edom."

This was the clue Nelson had found in his Bible describing the seaport used by the wealthy and wise king as headquarters for his far-flung trading operations. Strangely enough, these are the only words in the Bible mentioning Solomon's harbor. While many paragraphs tell of the king's fabulous enterprises during Israel's most glorious period and enumerate the exotic products brought from faraway countries by the royal sailing vessels, nothing is said about the port opening on the vital sea lanes to the lands of spices and gold with which Solomon traded so actively.

Continuing on the path opened by Fritz Frank, and trusting in his own dating of the potsherds, Nelson decided on the site of Tell el-Kheleifeh for his excavation. On this spot at the southern tip of the Wadi Arabah, facing the Gulf of Aqabah, he and his American colleagues endured great discomfort. For the next three seasons— from 1938 to 1940—the team worked, ate, and slept in biting winds and blinding sandstorms. During that time they excavated a large complex of buildings. Among their findings was a smelting furnace which Nelson, for a long time, believed to be of Solomonic origin. Later research proved that the smelter did not belong to that era. But when large copper and iron nails, pitch,

74

and remnants of nautical rope were found, the men knew they were on the right track at last. Apparently the site had been a large shipyard where Solomon's seagoing vessels were built and loaded for their long journeys.

Not until his third and last season of digging did Nelson have reason to think that he had actually found Ezion-geber, the town which was called Elath in the years after the reign of Solomon. This name—Eilat, in its modern version—it has kept to this day. His belief was borne out during a walk along the seaward side of the excavation. There he noticed an entranceway amid the rubble of a once formidable wall. This, he felt, must have been an original entrance that had led into the heart of Ezion-geber. Had an enemy planned to invade the town, he would have needed to pass through three separate gates, one built behind the other, for this triple-locked entrance had separate guardrooms with an individual complement of soldiers to guard each gate.

Familiar with other Palestinian excavations, Nelson knew that the heavily guarded triple entrance was a unique feature of Solomonic fortifications. He compared his findings to the building plans of other cities connected with the Solomonic era, and decided he had found the king's seaport. With the knowledge available to him, it seemed right to identify his discovery as belonging to the time of the great king. He knew he had found a seaport. Whether Tell el-Kheleifeh was actually Ezion-geber remained to be seen. Confirming his theory, however, Nelson noted that the heavy walls he had excavated at Tell el-Kheleifeh were constructed in a manner that matched other Solomonic structures. The special way in which the bricks were laid, the bonding of each wall to the other—these were trademarks of the king's building style. To Nelson's knowledge, neither before nor after Solomon's time was masonry thus constructed.

Apparently King Solomon had had a great gift for

finding foreign talent to be used to his advantage. During his reign the Phoenicians—his congenial neighbors to the northwest—were the world's expert shipbuilders and sailors. It was probably they who were responsible for the dynamic operations of the royal trading ships. Laden with the smelted copper and iron of the Wadi Arabah, these sailing ships departed from Ezion-geber, bound for Ophir (East Africa?) and other distant points. After a journey of three years' length they returned to their home port, their holds bulging with the marvelous cargos of which the Bible speaks: "gold, and silver, ivory, and apes, and peacocks."

Into Ezion-geber had come the building materials for Solomon's Temple, the sanctuary which would forever establish Jerusalem as a city of holiness. Cedar and cypress wood from Lebanon was transshipped through Ezion-geber, and when boatloads of gold, silver, and ivory from Africa arrived there, an especially gifted craftsman, Hiram of Tyre, was engaged to fashion the precious metals into the dazzling furnishings that made Solomon's Temple the showplace of the realm.

Not only ships traveled to Ezion-geber. It was during King Solomon's lifetime that camels first became the desert beast of burden, changing the whole mode of commerce in the East. Camels were not as dependent on water as donkeys, and because travel was no longer limited to the distance between water holes it became faster. Camels carried heavier loads than donkeys, increasing the volume of trade considerably.

Both goods and passengers had to pass Ezion-geber on their journey, for Israel lay at the northern end of the Incense Road from Arabia. It was important to have the good will of the king of Israel in these transactions: all merchandise bound for Egypt, Syria, and Phoenicia had to travel through his lands.

The camel caravans which traveled the trade routes of the Orient brought new and strange merchandise from unknown parts of the world. They also became carriers of information, spreading the news about the broad-minded and clever ruler of Israel to other Oriental lands.

Perhaps it was through such couriers that the Queen of Sheba first heard about Solomon and his fabulous and peaceful empire.

Curious to see for herself, she equipped a caravan, richly laden with her country's finest exports of perfumes, spices, and gold. Leaving her kingdom behind her (today experts believe North Yemen to be the site of ancient Sheba), the adventurous lady traveled northward through the Arabian desert along the Red Sea coastal route, a distance of some 1,250 miles. When her camel train reached Ezion-geber, the long journey through the Negev to Jerusalem still lay ahead. But the heartland of Israel was well defended by royal troops. The Queen of Sheba, intent on furthering trade relations, may have felt safer on this stretch than during all of the rest of her arduous business trip.

In 1937, during his first season at Tell el-Kheleifeh, Nelson found fragments of a large jar. He and his helpers were able to put it together and restore its original shape as a container of some precious product. Several of the fragments were inscribed with an ancient script. The script was identified as Minaean. The Minaeans were a South Arabian people known to be among the world's oldest traders. It was they who controlled the Incense Route with their main specialties of myrrh and frankincense. It was quite possible, as Nelson noted, that the jar he found in the sand of Tell el-Kheleifeh resembled some of the containers in which the Queen of Sheba brought her expensive presents to her appointment in Jerusalem.

With his momentous discoveries at Tell el-Kheleifeh,

Nelson laid bare the heart of the biblical stories concerning the fabulous reign of King Solomon; archaeology had substantiated many of his theories. When he wrote his official expedition report on the three seasons of work, Nelson had the enormous satisfaction of having shed some light on historical facts which had until his time been considered more legendary than believable.

The discovery of "King Solomon's Mines" had much popular appeal. The name of Nelson Glueck and his findings became known not only to his colleagues in the profession, but to thousands of armchair archaeologists who were to read his books, *The Other Side of the Jordan* and *Rivers in the Desert.*

By the end of his last season at Tell el-Kheleifeh, Nelson had located four different towns at that site. He did not doubt that the first—and greatest—town belonged to the Solomonic period and had been built by the king's engineers. Three subsequent levels of occupation rested on top of the Solomonic remains. One was Judaean, the other two were Edomite towns from the period when the site became known as Elath.

Looking for a seaport, Nelson had found an important industrial town as well. These two discoveries were major achievements in themselves. To Nelson they were important clues to the story of the area which apply to the history of Israel to this day.

It became more apparent than ever, as a result of our excavations, why Edom and Judah had fought so long and so bitterly with each other over the Arabah and Ezion-geber. . . . The copper and iron mines of the Arabah and the control of access to the Red Sea were as much a cause of inextinguishable rivalry between them as oil in Arabia and along the Persian Gulf is a source of competi-

tion and conflict among many nations today. . . .
Domination of the Wadi Arabah and Ezion-geber
and thus of the land and sea-routes which led to the
spices and gold and precious products of Arabia
and Africa and India was of life and death importance to them. Free access to the Gulf of
Aqabah and the undisturbed right of innocent
passage through it, are of no less importance to the
modern states bordering it.

Nelson was sorry to see the excavations at Ezion-geber
come to an end. There was much more he wanted to find
out, but again, time was running out. He had the feeling
that this might have been his most important project so
far, certainly the most richly rewarding, in "tying up the
threads of history."

He had developed a fondness, almost a personal
affection, for this part of Israel, especially since he had
invested so much of himself here. Almost at the very last
minute of the last day before the expedition was to break
up, Nelson decided on an inspection—a farewell tour of
the site. With him went the Arab foreman who had
worked with the expedition during its three seasons at
Tell el-Kheleifeh.

The excavation had torn down almost every bit of the
site; little of anything was left standing. But Nelson
noticed a small piece of one mud-brick wall which had
been left untouched, poking out of the general rubble of
the site. He asked the foreman to knock it over with his
pickaxe. When the man did, he saw a tiny object lying in
the sand which he quickly picked up. Nelson saw it too,
and asked the foreman, Abbas, what he had found. Half-
joking, Abbas asked whether he would still receive
baksheesh for it since the excavation was now officially
closed.

I told Abbas that I would be delighted to pay him baksheesh, even at this stage of the game. He persisted and asked if I were willing to pay as much as a shilling or two for what he held in his closed fist.

"Hand it over, Abbas," I said to him. He gave it to me. I took a hurried look, stuck it into an inner pocket, and told him to hold out his hands in cupped form. With that, I emptied into them all the silver and paper money in my pockets. It may have been the equivalent of fifty dollars. It was a lot of money for that part of the world. I could have easily engineered a minor revolution with it. He looked at the heap of shillings and pounds, which was indeed a veritable fortune to him, and after a moment, said to me: "Ya Mudir (O Master), but I can't possibly take all that money from you."

I assured him that I thought what he had found was worth a good reward, and that anyway I had intended giving him a parting gift. He had been most faithful and helpful during the years we had worked together, and we had become good friends. We embraced and took leave of each other, he back to Aqabah and the rest of us to our cars on the way to Amman and Jerusalem.

That last-minute discovery turned out to be of some importance in bearing out Nelson's interpretation of the history of Ezion-geber. It was a seal-signet ring that had once belonged to a Judaean king, and the only one of its type so far found.

It was the kind of seal which an important personage, possibly an official, wore on his belt. Nelson studied it with curiosity. A ram with horns standing behind the figure of a man was engraved on its stone. Above the

Oil lamp found by Nelson Glueck during the excavation of Tell el-Kheleifeh.

Seal-signet ring found at Tell el-Kheleifeh expedition, and assumed to have belonged to a royal governor after the reign of King Solomon.

figures three Hebrew letters spelled out the name
"Jotham" in reverse. The letter L, meaning "belonging
to," preceded the name.

This ring might have belonged to a royal governor
ruling over Elath in the period after Ezion-geber had
fallen into ruins. A King Jotham had reigned over Judah
years after the death of King Solomon. As Nelson held the
ring in his hand, he wondered if it hadn't once been the
governor's official badge of office, the token by which he
ruled over the town before it dropped into the shadows of
history.

"For the Lord thy God bringeth thee into a good land
. . . a land whose stones are iron, and out of whose hills
thou mayest dig brass." How right he had been to follow
those guiding words. The importance of his discoveries
even Nelson could not foretell on that day he said goodbye
to Tell el-Kheleifeh.

Recently copper has once more been mined in the same
area by Israelis who toil proudly in the mines that once
belonged to King Solomon. The city of Eilat, which made
Nelson Glueck an honorary citizen, has become a great
mecca for travelers from all over the world. These tourists
marvel to find themselves in the town once visited by that
famous earlier traveler, the Queen of Sheba, and proudly
carry home souvenirs fashioned out of malachite, the
"Eilat Stone."

Nelson hoped to return to Tell el-Kheleifeh someday
for further work, but now, as he turned his back on
Solomon's seaport, he was also eager to reach Jerusalem,
where some important personal business awaited him.

9

NELSON SAT AT HIS DESK on the third floor of the Iglauer house, which had been turned into a study for him, and looked out over the ice-covered branches of the tall trees hugging the house in wintry embrace. Now that he was home for good, he spent much time up here surrounded by his pottery and the many notes scattered over his worktable and bookshelves. He spent hours here each night, typing away. Writing, for him, was a great pleasure. No matter how late the hour, part of every day was given over to his session at the typewriter.

With the war raging in Europe and no chance of digging in Palestine for the duration, Nelson consoled himself with his teaching at Hebrew Union College and the many publications and magazine articles he was turning out. In front of him, standing on a corner of the desk, was a copy of his first book, *The Other Side of the Jordan*, which had been published by the American School and had appeared just at the time of his return to America. It bore the dedication, "To Helen and Charles Jonathan," and Nelson felt that his wife more than deserved it.

In the autumn of 1939 Nelson had lectured widely throughout America on topics resulting from his archaeological expeditions. He had found enormous acceptance from his audiences when he talked about his explorations in Transjordan, Moab, and Edom, pictured the hardships and glories of finding "King Solomon's

Copper Mines," or discussed the uses of biblical archaeology. It was Helen who felt that less scholarly groups
would also be interested in what Nelson had to tell about
his work. This also applied to his writing, so much of
which was strictly scientific and professional. "Why don't
you write something I can read?" she said to her husband.
She thought his material would make very good reading,
especially if written in a more popular vein.

Nelson listened to her. When some of his colleagues at
the American School in Jerusalem also urged him to write
down his experiences, he enlarged several of his lectures,
rewrote them in a less scientific manner, and added
photographs which showed the reader what he was
talking about. *The Other Side of the Jordan* was finished
in March of 1940 and became the first of Nelson's
publications intended for the nonprofessional reader.

It was not a strange feeling to be home, but it was the
longest he had ever been away from Jerusalem, and he
had a bad case of homesickness for that city. He had been
gone more than a year now, and who knew when or how
he could return?

He recalled praying in the chapel of Hadassah Hospital
not long after his auspicious homecoming from Eilat and
the conclusion of the Ezion-geber project. Helen was
having surgery, and Nelson, extremely worried, prayed
for a happy outcome to her ordeal and steady hands for
Dr. Zondek, the renowned surgeon, who was attending
her. And he remembered how later, in Helen's room on
the maternity floor, the nurse's starched skirt had rustled
as she held out a well-wrapped bundle to him.

"Meet your son, Professor Glueck. He's a big, strapping fellow . . . with a voice to match."

Nelson had bent over the baby sleeping in the arms of
the nurse. It was a surprise to him to see a beautiful little
boy, light-haired and healthy, and he had been speech-

less. Overcome by emotion and relief, the tall, dignified man stood, tears streaming down his cheeks at the first sight of his son.

From her bed Helen had smiled, knowing what this moment meant to him. He had waited for his son, not wanting to interfere with her internship and hospital residency by starting a family before she was ready. With his own frequent absences from home, he knew what an important part of her life Helen's medical career was. He respected her success as a physician and was immensely proud of her.

Before the baby's arrival they had selected the name Charles Jonathan, in case it was a boy. This was to commemorate Helen's brother, Charles Iglauer, who had died at age twenty-one. Now Nelson teased Helen.

"Dr. Glueck, will our son become a physician like his mother?"

"I wouldn't mind if he became a famous archaeologist like his father," laughed Helen.

But both of them were struck by the baby's amazing resemblance to Helen's father, Dr. Sam Iglauer, and joked about the future fourth-generation Iglauer physician who was that night sleeping in the nursery of Hadassah Hospital.

They had chosen Judah and Beatrice Magnes to be Charles Jonathan's godparents and were delighted when they consented. Of the many people Nelson and Helen Glueck knew in Jerusalem, they felt closest to Rabbi and Mrs. Magnes. Neighbors in the Herod's Gate quarter of East Jerusalem, both Magneses had given Helen much loving attention during the time Nelson was away, and she had felt comforted by their presence only a few streets away. It was good to know of their closeness whenever she had felt isolated in the mixed section of Arabs, Jews, and Christians, where almost no English was spoken.

Rabbi Judah L. Magnes was the American-born first president of Hebrew University. He was an ardent Zionist who had chosen early to live in Palestine. In the beginning 1920s he left behind a distinguished career as an American clergyman and educator and made *aliyah* with his wife and children. He was a man with a dream. As a dynamic pacifist he had worked on behalf of peace during his time as rabbi of several prominent American congregations. Saddened by the outbreak of the First World War, he went to Europe and aided in massive war relief programs there.

When he settled in Jerusalem it became his life's ambition to be among the group of dedicated men who were building up an institution of higher learning there. It was hoped this institution would bring about a renaissance of Jewish culture in the city which had meant most to Jews throughout their history. When in 1925 he was one of the founders who dedicated Hebrew University on Mount Scopus, one of his dreams came true. It was but the beginning of many years spent in the service of this institution of higher Jewish learning.

Nelson remembered walking beside the older man in silence, one Jerusalem morning full of promise, as they were climbing the steep road leading up the hill to where Hebrew University stood. It was a walk Nelson took often when he was in Jerusalem. He loved accompanying Judah Magnes to his office, for his friend was an intrepid walker too, and in the forty-five minutes it took from their homes in East Jerusalem to reach the office of the university president, much could be talked about.

A spectacular view of Jerusalem lay beneath them as they reached the top of the mountain. Surrounded by the city walls, narrow crooked streets, and church towers, the magnificent golden Dome of the Rock glinted in the sunlight below.

"Look at this beautiful and serene city," Magnes's voice quivered with dramatic intensity. For an instant it was possible to picture him as the vibrant, stirring rabbi who had fired his New York congregations with the sermons he preached to them. "People could live here together in permanent peace if they only tried."

Nelson nodded. He was acquainted with Magnes's favorite hope of establishing a joint Arab-Jewish state. With unlimited immigration for anyone wishing to live in Palestine, both Jews and Arabs would exist here side by side, ruled by a government which promised equality to all. Nelson had heard his friend propose such a settlement at many a meeting of highly placed Mandate officials and important Arabs. Judah Magnes could be highly persuasive at such gatherings; he was listened to with great respect.

Nelson kicked aside a small pebble with his foot. At this point total peace seemed a beautiful, unattainable dream. The fulfillment of their hopes for an independent state in Palestine would have to await the good will and permission of leading European governments whose problems were more urgent and pressing at the moment.

"I am sending Helen and the baby home next week," Nelson said softly.

A look of pain crossed the handsome Magnes face fleetingly. "Yes," he agreed, "it'll be difficult to find shipboard accommodations once war breaks out. You, too, will have to think about getting back."

They had reached the portal of Hebrew University, but Magnes was not yet ready to go in and motioned to Nelson that they should walk on a little farther. So they headed southward, passing the university, and strolled toward a spot from where they had a wide-ranging view of the Wilderness of Judah. It was a clear day, and they could see as far south as the shores of the Dead Sea. Far off in the distance, the hills of Moab and Edom melted away in a purplish tint, merging with the soft edges of the shoreline.

"I have a great deal of work here," mused Nelson, "tying up loose ends on the Transjordan survey, finishing up the expedition report, shipping home statuary for the Cincinnati Museum. I really can't get away yet."

"It would serve little purpose to have you caught here in a war, Nelson. In America you could do more good for all of us."

It was unreal to think of war amid this tranquil morning scene. One southward glance from here and Nelson realized anew how much he was part of this land. His heart was here, and he wished he could spend the rest of his life here too, without the frequent goodbyes and departures of his current existence. He knew what mysteries those far-off hills held. His hands had touched the relics left behind by ancient tribesmen whose civilization had vanished long ago. The tale the potsherds told had become a part of his own life. But much remained for him to investigate. Even the length of his days would not be long enough to find out all he wanted to know.

"I was in Tel-Aviv yesterday. I met some survivors who escaped the British patrols when their Turkish freighter blew up near Haifa. Forty-five days in the hold of a decrepit fruit steamer and then they were forbidden to land here . . . " Magnes's voice broke off.

Now that Poland had fallen to Hitler's troops no one around Jerusalem doubted the dire fate awaiting any Jews caught in the German net. For Judah Magnes these were days of torment. For a long time he had tried to use his well-connected British friends to ease the ban on Jewish immigration into Palestine. While others made frantic preparations to smuggle in refugees right under the noses of the British, Magnes tried to help his close friend

Henrietta Szold in her efforts to rescue and bring to Palestine as many Jewish children as could still be gotten out of Europe.

"No one wanted them," Magnes was saying, his eyes looking at, but not seeing, the serene vista ahead of him. "That little ship stopped at every port between Genoa and Haifa, but no country allowed anyone to disembark. There were many suicides aboard; others died of diseases and the dreadful food. But most of the passengers still believed they would be allowed to enter once they actually got to Palestine. Seven hundred people were aboard that ship when it sailed into Haifa harbor." He suddenly stopped, unable to continue his story.

Every day new tales circulated throughout Jerusalem and Tel-Aviv about the ships loaded with European refugees that were intercepted by the British. This latest story had everyone's blood boiling. In the sight of relatives and friends who had come down to the docks to welcome the newcomers, British guns had ordered the ship to turn around and leave port. Knowing what awaited them should they be returned to German hands, the desperate passengers had made their last move for freedom. As the small steamer sailed out, the onlookers saw black smoke hover over her. Then followed a sudden explosion. No one on shore would ever forget the sight of the slowly sinking boat, scuttled by its passengers, who were now jumping overboard. Many of them drowned right there in the waters off the Palestinian shore.

In the December grayness of the Sunday afternoon, Nelson stood at his window and thought about his friend from whom he was now so far away. He experienced again a feeling of satisfaction that Judah Magnes thought of him so highly. Nelson had always appreciated the friendship of his fellow American—a Reform Jew like him—who loved Palestine with a similar passion. Magnes's every word and action dealt with the growth and future of the Holy Land. Nelson remembered that his friend, finding delight in Nelson's archaeological work, had several times asked to be allowed to come along on field trips. And he was pleased when Magnes praised his talent for organizing expeditions.

In his mind he saw Magnes again on the day they had watched the splendid view of the Judaean mountains together. The older man's glance had rested on him. "Don't take it lightly, Nelson," he heard Magnes say close to his shoulder, "the day will come when you, as a leader, will be able to give us invaluable help. What you see here now will impress upon you the work that needs to be done—the enormous job of uniting the American Jewish community, the propaganda that will help us live, the fund-raising. Someday much of it will be done by you or under your direction. And I know of no one who will do the job better."

He had walked Magnes back to the university, and at the president's office he had taken leave of his friend. With a last backward glance at the countryside that meant so much to him, Nelson had started the long walk down from Mount Scopus and headed for the American School.

It was August 1940 before Nelson decided to leave. Helen and baby Charles had already returned to Cincinnati, but this time Nelson barely made it back home to America. By then travel westward through the Mediterranean was cut off—no ship dared sail this route any longer. Knowing that no new explorations would be possible because of the war, Nelson left the American School in the hands of another American archaeologist and headed for home via the eastern route, little dreaming what an odyssey his journey would become. From Jerusalem he was driven to Baghdad, where he stayed a day before "a sort of

Toonerville Trolley railway car" got him as far as Basra, Iraq. A small steamer provided passage down the Persian Gulf to Karachi, Pakistan, and on to Bombay, India, where Nelson found an American freighter which took him to Johannesburg, South Africa, and afterwards to Trinidad, before arriving in New York City. By the time Nelson saw home again he had sailed on the Arabian Sea, the Indian Ocean, the South Atlantic Ocean and the North Atlantic, and the journey had taken seven weeks.

After such an adventure it seemed tame to be teaching undergraduates again. Europe was in flames, people everywhere were fleeing the Germans, to whom one country after another fell. Nelson, pacing his third-floor study on a Sunday afternoon in December, stopped. He thought he heard unusual noises downstairs in the kitchen, where dinner preparations were underway— loud voices, as if someone had turned the radio up too high. Then he heard fast steps on the staircase. Helen was half running upstairs, and in a moment her face, pale and shocked, appeared in his doorway.

"Nelson," her voice was excited at the news, "Pearl Harbor has just been bombed by the Japanese."

10

NOT MANY MONTHS after America entered the war, Nelson received a long-distance call at his office at Hebrew Union College in Cincinnati.

"Dr. Glueck, this is the Office of Strategic Services in Washington. Our director would like to see you as quickly as possible. When do you think you could get here?"

From the little he knew about the OSS, Nelson was aware that this little-publicized government agency gathered vital information to help the war effort, and that most of its activities were of a highly secret and dangerous nature. Intrigued by such a mysterious summons, Nelson arrived in Washington within twenty-four hours of the call.

As he stepped through a door marked COL. WILLIAM J. DONOVAN in small black-painted letters, he was still wondering what this visit was all about and why an American spy organization was interested in a professor of biblical archaeology.

After a special flight via South America and Central Africa, the U.S. Air Force plane landed in Cairo and deposited its one civilian passenger. From Cairo the civilian continued his trip by private plane to the outskirts of Jerusalem.

Before long an astonished staff at the American School of Oriental Research stared, then welcomed back its former director, who had been assumed to be in America for the "duration."

Nelson, relaxed and happy, grinned at their surprise. He was just as delighted to be back as they were to see him. He was more than ready to resume the work he had so unwillingly left behind when he was forced to leave Jerusalem in August 1940. Of course, no one asked him how he had managed to return. Or why he had come back during a time of critical warfare which now engulfed most of the Mediterranean.

Nelson assumed direction of the American School again, also acting as field director of the Baghdad branch of the school.

Almost all archaeological work in the Near East had stopped because of the war, and many of Nelson's former colleagues had been recalled to assume war duties. Nelson was almost alone in the field now.

Undisturbed he roamed the desert again, searching patiently for the potsherds which marked the ancient village sites he recorded on his empty map. Every night he visited the nearest Arab encampment and received the typical Oriental hospitality accorded to strangers.

He sat in the tents of the local sheiks, joked with his hosts in true man-to-man fashion, and shared the feasts of the Bedouins. But there were also times when he broke bread with poor tribesmen who, with the pride of wealthy potentates, invited him to partake of their frugal meal of pitta, eggs, and tea.

It went unnoticed among his hosts that Nelson listened sharply to local gossip while he was among them. It did not matter to them that he was just as interested in the present as in the past history of the desert. They were delighted to have a visitor with whom they could indulge in their favorite sport: talking.

Often Nelson asked questions. Sometimes he inquired

how they felt about the big war that was now close to them, in North Africa. When his hosts told him that other "visitors" had come by and asked questions, Nelson gathered that German spies were operating in the area.

In this free and genial exchange of pleasantries, none of the local Arabs suspected that the skinny American professor who rode his camel through the blazing desert sands, picked up useless, broken pieces of old pottery, and regaled them with jokes in his funny-accented Arabic was looking for more than ancient history.

For Nelson's work these painful years of war were fruitful. He persevered in the exacting mapping of Transjordan's past, for he considered the time he was allowed to spend here a personal gift. He disciplined himself not to squander it. Often the temperature exceeded 110 degrees and it took extreme self-control to get through a working day in the desert. Even the native guides admired Nelson's stamina.

Except for the highlands, much of Transjordan consisted of flat lands. There were few tells here. Finding no hills to oppose them, the strong winds of the desert had worn down all levels of human habitation to dust which had long since been carried away.

But the pottery fragments remained. And their shapes and markings, and sometimes their inscriptions, told Nelson enough. They told him that towns had once stood here, what type of people had lived in them, and why the sites had been abandoned long ago.

Nelson observed more than most people. He had the training of the archaeologist, which enabled him to find artifacts and visualize the people who had used them. He had an excellent knowledge of biblical and historical sources. And he had a talent for picturing in words what he saw and what he imagined.

During the day he walked the land and investigated its

hills and valleys. At night he rested on its soil. He examined archaeological sites, but it was the story of people and ideas that drew him to the past.

He saw more than a ruined fortress; he pictured the savage battle that had raged here before the victor torched the town, taking away its inhabitants as enslaved captives.

A long-deserted mine told him of precious metals once molten here to serve as embellishment for the Holy Temple in Jerusalem, of a kingdom enlightened and wealthy whose fame was legendary throughout the ancient world.

A road through the desert conjured up countless generations of caravaneers plodding across it throughout the centuries.

It was Nelson's firm belief that the ground he was treading was the most important in the long history of the world. It was not only the geographical center of the earth. The three major Western religions had sprung from this spiritual "heartland."

In his travels through the Jordan Valley, the birthplace of Judaism and Christianity, Nelson became even more impressed with the remarkable influence of this small piece of earth on the story of mankind.

> Palestine's blessing and curse lie in its geographical position, which makes it a bridge between the nations. It is a crossroads on the deathless trade routes between East and West. Its strategic importance in more recent times has been recognized and fought over by Richard the Lionhearted and Saladin, by Napoleon and Nelson, by Allenby and Liman von Sanders, by Wavell and Rommel. It stands today between England and India, between America and Arabia, whose desert sands cover an ocean of oil.

In his Washington office Colonel William Donovan of the OSS looked very pleased. On the glass-topped desk before him lay a perfect series of aerial photos which outlined in detail the terrain of Transjordan. This latest piece of intelligence had just reached him from "his man" in Jerusalem, and the colonel studied it intently.

Map in hand, Colonel Donovan walked over to the huge global war charts lining one wall of his office. He picked up a pointer and with it traced a slow, thoughtful line on the wall map. Beginning in Egypt, his pointer crossed the Gulf of Aqabah at Eilat, then pursued a long, northward trek through the Wadi Arabah into Syria and stopped at the border of Turkey. Frequently the colonel referred to the photo map in his hand. This "archaeological" map was the best reconnaissance study the British Royal Air Force had ever made. It was a real "scoop" that his agent's friendship with a British "big wig" had paid off so well. Little could the unknown friend suspect that this very map might help British troops get out of a real hot spot some day.

As President Roosevelt's secret emissary to many wartime leaders, "Wild Bill" Donovan knew more about the war's conduct than many a general. And he fervently hoped that the British soldiers now fighting Rommel's Afrika Korps in Egypt would defeat the Germans before they reached the Suez Canal. Because if they did not, Colonel Donovan knew that the photograph he was holding might be the only salvation left the British "Tommies" in their escape from the "Desert Fox."

Returning to his desk the colonel put down the aerial photographs. It was a strange quirk that the emergency plans for evacuating British troops should have been thought out by the discoverer of King Solomon's copper mines. Even stranger that parts of the evacuation route had once been used by King Solomon's soldiers.

Colonel Donovan's mouth, usually grim when reflecting news of the war, wore a slight grin. Ever since he had read about Nelson Glueck's exploits, he had wondered how he could utilize the archaeologist's great wealth of information about the Middle East. And now he had brought the two together: Nelson Glueck and the Allied war effort. What a delightful maneuver.

Professor Glueck, on an archaeological survey spanning all of Transjordan, had the perfect cover for his mission. No other person knew the territory the way Glueck did: every mile was a personal acquaintance. Who would dream that while he was digging up ancient villages the famous explorer was mapping out escape routes for the British Army?

As he worked his way through Transjordan, Nelson discovered over twelve hundred sites that had once been populated towns and villages. It was an unheard-of feat. No previous explorer had scanned a whole country so thoroughly and systematically. This solid scientific record did honor to his profession. His research opened new windows on the past.

Throughout the years of World War II Nelson lived— and enjoyed—an adventurous double existence. As a hardworking archaeologist, he made discoveries which surpassed all previous knowledge about a land that had so far been only a "blank space on a historical map." At the same time, as an agent of the OSS, he operated in "cloak-and-dagger" secrecy, keeping his eyes and ears alerted for information which could help his government, and which he transmitted in the special code he had learned during his brief interview in Washington.

But there was another paradox to the war years, and a person as thoughtful and sensitive as Nelson could not fail to be aware of it and be moved.

As he dug deeper into the past, tracing out the history

of the people in the Holy Land, he was helping to build a foundation for the study of human civilization. Each time he concluded a field trip and returned to Jerusalem, tragic news of the present awaited him. One by one the Jewish communities of Europe—Poland, Russia, France, Belgium, Romania, Greece—were destroyed by the German murder machine. The descendants of Abraham and Moses—his own people—were swallowed up in this horrendous whirlwind. The true cost in Jewish lives had not yet leaked to the outside world. Nelson, as a Jew and a rabbi, grieved over the oppression of his people and the total destruction of their ancient institutions of worship and learning in Europe.

Nelson breathed easier when the last of the Axis forces in North Africa surrendered to Allied troops and the fighting shifted to the European continent. No one who knew him or worked with him at the American School had any idea of his secret mission. And he was glad that his alternate plan for an Allied escape route had become only a theoretical exercise which never needed to be used.

His experience as a secret agent had confirmed to Nelson how right he was to consider Palestine the heartland of the world. He decided to write another book.

In *The River Jordan* Nelson's enormous knowledge of biblical and historical information, the timeless quality of the land, and his own poetic gift are melted together to restore events that had once occurred in this area of "The Gardens of God."

The River Jordan was published in 1946. In the following year the Transjordan survey, too, came to an end. At last the war was over and Nelson had arrived at the crossroads of a new chapter in his life. He reached this point exactly at the time when the true toll of the Holocaust came to light and the world learned how almost complete had been the extermination of European Jewry. The partition of Palestine and the birth of a Jewish state were still only remote possibilities.

Both crucial phenomena lay heavily on the minds of Jewish leaders during those days. Nelson was preparing to leave Jerusalem to return to his teaching job in Cincinnati. He was unable to start any new research project in Palestine because of the renewed Arab hostilities, during which even *he* would not be safe.

The enormity of the European catastrophe burdened Nelson's soul. It seemed to him that the Jews in the Western Hemisphere now had a binding duty to carry on the Jewish culture and learning which the Holocaust had left in ashes, for if they did not, Hitler's boast of "closing the door" on Judaism would truly come to pass.

During these turbulent days in Jerusalem, Nelson received a letter from Cincinnati which was to change the direction of his life. Would he consider the presidency of Hebrew Union College?

Nelson Glueck, his wife and child, pictured in Jerusalem during his tenure as Director of the American School of Oriental Research, 1947.

11

NELSON ACCEPTED the presidency of Hebrew Union College at a time of great crisis in Jewish affairs. In Europe Jewish life had come to a full stop. In Palestine Jews were struggling to bring a new country into the world amid dire predictions that it would never come to be. If Judaism had any chance to revive and grow, it would have to happen in America.

In the chapel of Hebrew Union College, an overflow crowd of students and invited guests forgot the raw March weather long enough to watch the inauguration of a new president, the fourth in the long history of America's oldest rabbinical school.

In black academic robes, head bowed, his long, slender fingers interlaced in an arch close to his chest, Nelson sat listening to his friend, Rabbi Joshua Loth Liebman of Boston, who delivered the sermon of consecration in Nelson's honor.

Nelson's face mirrored his gravely serious feelings. When retiring Dr. Julian Morgenstern shook his hand at the end of the ceremony, no one failed to read the implications of the gesture. Nelson's former teacher was turning over the school's leadership to his one-time student. That was a credit to them both. But the enormous responsibilities which the new position brought—at a most difficult time—these were for Nelson to handle alone.

As he took the measure of the tasks ahead of him, members of the Board of Governors congratulated themselves. A man of international scientific repute, a scholar respected equally by Jew and Gentile, a man who would handle delicate administrative problems with sensitivity—they were highly pleased with their choice.

"I am a native of Cincinnati," he had said to them at their first meeting, "but I am a spiritual son of Jerusalem." It sounded poetic. It sounded fitting for a man of such international and liberal scope. But those whom he addressed learned quickly that Nelson meant it. It was his credo.

Of all the guests witnessing Nelson's consecration, only Helen really knew that her husband did not accept his high position with eagerness. She alone knew he would have preferred to devote his full strength to the pursuit of archaeology, that his real true love lay in the soil of the Holy Land.

But Nelson was not one to turn down a challenge. The presidency of an institution like the Hebrew Union College was not to be taken lightly. Now that America had become the wealthiest, most heavily populated center of Jewish life—the only such nucleus left in the world—its theological schools functioned as spiritual guides to the whole American Jewish community.

Judah Magnes had pointed this out to Nelson when he heard about the letter from Cincinnati. He reminded his friend and protege that it was his duty to accept the mandate that had come his way.

"This is your chance to serve, Nelson," Magnes had pronounced with dramatic persuasion, "the time of building for the future has come." And Nelson, convinced that he must not turn down such an influential position during a time of peril, had accepted the new job as a college president.

Nelson thought of Judah Magnes on his consecration day, and of the huge compliment his friend had paid him. It was a great responsibility Nelson was about to begin. But if it was Magnes's opinion that he was the perfect man for the position, Nelson would do his very best to prove his mentor right.

He began almost immediately. At the lavish festive dinner given at a large Cincinnati hotel in honor of the incoming president of Hebrew Union College, Nelson rose for an unscheduled announcement.

It was a great personal pleasure, he said, that he could inform his friends of the impending lecture series by the almost legendary Rabbi Leo Baeck, courageous leader of Berlin's Jewish community, who had survived self-imposed exile with his people at the Theresienstadt concentration camp. Leo Baeck would teach the students at HUC during the coming year while in residence on their campus.

Murmurs of astonishment rose up in the banquet hall. Even Helen, sitting beside him on the dais, looked at Nelson in amazement. She knew nothing of this. When had Nelson made the arrangements? And where would he get the funds for such an illustrious visitor to the College? Her husband smiled when she whispered her questions to him a little later.

"So far there is neither an agreement nor are there funds," he whispered back. "It was an idea I just had. But it will work out . . . somehow."

The *somehow* became reality, one of the many *somehows* that were to pop up during his years as president. "Do it now" was Nelson's motto, applied to every important decision. If it was important enough for the College, he did not mind asking people for help. And he did not have much trouble finding help. The persuasiveness of his charming manner was a great asset in raising funds for projects he deemed worthy. People could not do enough for him.

Rabbi Leo Baeck did come to Cincinnati that year, giving up retirement in England and important writing long enough to teach the young. His well-kept goatee and the snowy-white vest that was his trademark became an accepted sight on the HUC campus, and many a seminary student benefited from hearing the great modern sage lecture on the ethics of Judaism.

It was an immense personal sorrow for Nelson when Judah Magnes died in October of 1948. His friend had been privileged to witness the birth of the State of Israel during that same year, but the violent warfare that erupted on the day following the announcement of statehood lay heavily on his heart during the last days of his life.

Nelson announced another important innovation while his friend was still alive. It was his hope, Nelson declared, that future graduates of Hebrew Union College would spend one year of their studies in Israel. This declaration brought great joy to the heart of Judah Magnes, who learned of it while on a visit home to America. It had been a lifetime dream of Magnes "that the rabbis and teachers of Judaism from all over the world could come to Jerusalem to find there the inspiration of the Hebrew renaissance." Now his disciple had taken the first step toward the fulfillment of his dream.

It was a time for building. This is how most people thought of Nelson Glueck's administration of Hebrew Union College. Under his leadership the school grew fast. Not even the Board of Governors and his closest colleagues on the faculty could foresee the whirlwind speed of growth during the years from 1948 to the early

1950s—or the formidable energies Nelson would devote to the College.

The scholar who loved the solitude of the desert turned into a first-class promoter. He became the best public relations expert the school could possibly have hired.

Ordaining new graduates, addressing public meetings, or persuading donors to invest in the school's future—he loved it all. It was part of Nelson's complex personality that he could be sparkling and scintillating in the company of people, and still be a man of intense solitude whose private meditations not even his intimates dared disturb.

Sometimes he remembered tales about Kovno where his uncle, Dov Revel, had lived and studied Torah in undisturbed concentration. Or he recalled the Berlin lecture halls where he had first heard Leo Baeck teach. That world was dead. But the tradition of learning had to be continued—in the new world. That was why Nelson wanted to build for the future.

Nelson felt that the American Jewish community was not sufficiently aware of its own background and history. It did not know its own roots or about the struggles of its pioneers. To learn of the part Jewish men and women had played in the building of America, to know about the sacrifices and the failures, along with the successes and achievements—*that* would instill a sense of pride in their heritage, such as European Jews had once known and fostered.

Jacob Marcus had his own favorite project which he suggested to the new president. Dr. Marcus, besides being a faculty member of the Hebrew Union College, was an eminent historian of early American Jewry. The material he had gathered for his studies was voluminous. The letters, documents, newspapers, and pictures he had so far brought together were priceless sources of information on the lives of early American Jews, and could be the beginning of a treasure house for students of American Jewish history. Why not make it available to anyone who sought this information?

This seemed an excellent idea to Nelson, and he charged Dr. Marcus with the creation of a national archives. The American Jewish Archives, housed on the Cincinnati campus of Hebrew Union College, today contains the largest collection of Jewish historical materials in this country. It is widely used by students of all denominations in their research.

Nelson was fortunate to have the complete support and help of his Board of Governors, who admired his determination to build for the future. With such eager backing many of his progressive ideas found expression.

During his presidency housing was found for the growing collection of Jewish art objects which the school had acquired over many years. The Hebrew Union College Museum contains many ritual and archaeological items which are proudly shown to all campus visitors. Courses on Jewish art, taught by world-famous authorities, also became a part of the school's curriculum.

When Hebrew Union College established an Interfaith Department, it opened the way for Christian ministers and scholars to become deeply acquainted with Jewish thought and Jewish subjects. It pleased Nelson that such a large number of non-Jewish students attended the school's postgraduate courses and received academic degrees. It proved to him something he had always felt strongly—that Jewish-Christian relations on a high level were needed—and are possible.

In 1948 Rabbi Stephen S. Wise announced his retirement from the Jewish Institute of Religion in New York. Twenty-five years earlier Rabbi Wise had founded his school for the training of young men as liberal Jewish ministers. Now he needed a successor to head the school.

Rabbi Wise was internationally famous for the many important roles he had played in the religious and social affairs of his people and his country. He pondered carefully the problem of entrusting his school to the leadership of a new man before he declared that Nelson Glueck must be the one.

To Stephen Wise, Nelson possessed all the qualities his school needed: he was a clergyman and a scholar, had a broad liberal spirit and an interest in interfaith relations, and was possessed by a deep love for Israel.

Of course, Nelson was flattered by the enormous compliment Rabbi Wise had paid him. Aware of New York's position as *the* center of America's largest Jewish population, he seized this golden chance to build up a large, influential organization.

The boards of both schools approved a merger. One important reason for this was that Nelson Glueck could now preside over both institutions and govern them as one. In October 1948 Nelson was installed in New York as the first president of the combined Hebrew Union College–Jewish Institute of Religion (HUC-JIR).

Not long afterwards Nelson suggested to his Board of Governors that Los Angeles, as the second-largest Jewish community in the country, might be an ideal site for a branch of the College-Institute. His colleagues agreed. In the early 1950s the California School was born and the College had another wing.

With such a strategic location of its three schools—in the East, the Middle West, and the West Coast—the College-Institute could now serve American Reform Jews, and the whole American Jewish community, more effectively than ever before.

If the first seat on the aisle, second pew, on the right side, was empty on a Friday night, everyone at the school knew

the president was out of the city. In the many long years of
his association with Hebrew Union College, Nelson never
missed a single Friday evening service at the Cincinnati
campus chapel if he could help it.

He sat beside his friend Jake Marcus and other
colleagues and ushered in the Sabbath amid the students.
Often this short religious service gave Nelson a few
precious moments of contemplation and peace that he was
rarely able to find during the rest of his busy week.

He listened as the young voices read their own prayers,
preached their sermons, and chanted the liturgies, both
old and new. Nelson found in these young men the
unbroken line of continuity from the past to the present.
Soon they would go out into the community life of
America and be rabbis, cantors, and teachers. In their
individual congregations they would pass on traditions,
teach the young, and in their own way respond to the
crises of their time. But it would all go on. Once more
Judaism would survive.

Countless generations of students respected and admired Nelson. Many were awed, even intimidated, by
him. He was a busy man due to his travels and commit-
ments, and it was not easy to become close to him, yet
there was a magnetism between them and him. Most of
them never knew how much they touched him, or that to
him they were a great source of hope for the future.

12

"I WOULD LIKE to see a string of towns built in the desert. From here to the Gulf of Aqabah," said David Ben-Gurion, raising his hand and pointing south.

They were walking together, the Prime Minister of Israel and Nelson, at Sde Boker, the kibbutz south of Beersheba which Ben-Gurion considered his home.

"You see, seventy percent of Israel's territory is right here in the wilderness, but our population lives mainly in the big cities. It is unwise to be clustered like that. We need a lifeline through the Negev like King Solomon had."

Impatiently Nelson had waited until he could return to Israel. Now that he was back, after the 1948 war, everything was different here. Israel had gained independence, but along with the joys of the long-dreamed-about homeland, she had assumed the problems of statehood. The most urgent of these was the need to protect the new state from attacks by her hostile neighbors.

In the glare of the desert sun, gentle breezes blew the famous stubborn white hair of Israel's leader, a tough and determined man who loved the desert as much as Nelson did. Together the two men stood at the edge of the kibbutz where the vastness of the Negev began. In looks they were different—Ben-Gurion, short and stubby, and Nelson, lank and tall—but two similarities attracted them to each other. Both shared an intense love for the land on which they stood, and both possessed an undisputable knowledge of the Bible.

From this knowledge of the Bible Ben-Gurion knew that returning the huge area of the Negev to human use was not a fantastic dream. It could be a reality. It might take the backbreaking labor and fierce devotion of his people, but it had been done before. That was why Ben-Gurion always enjoyed his conversations with Nelson Glueck, who knew first-hand that the Negev had once been livable.

Ben-Gurion felt that Israel would be more secure if the Negev were settled. Her neighbors, defeated in the fierce war which followed Israel's independence, were ever alert for a chance to resume their attacks. The empty regions of the desert provided convenient pockets for infiltrators.

Above all, Ben-Gurion wanted access to the Suez Canal. Israel had only one usable harbor, at Haifa. The use of Eilat as a back door for trade with the Orient was urgent to the safety and the nourishment of the new country.

Just as King Solomon, in his day, had installed fortified garrisons between his seaport of Ezion-geber and his capital, Jerusalem, Ben-Gurion now saw that populated settlements and towns in the Negev would safeguard the whole country.

From his conversations with Ben-Gurion and other officials, Nelson was convinced that he, as an archaeologist, could do his share in finding modern uses for the age-old secrets held by the Negev. He was eager to begin another expedition. Tensions in Palestine had prevented him from working on any major new project since the Transjordan survey. And he had missed those summers of digging.

Nelson, too, was to feel the postwar effects of politics. Transjordan was now the Kingdom of Jordan and off-limits to him. After all the years of scientific research he had done in the territory, Jordanian officials would not allow him back into their land. They considered him a spy for the Israelis.

Nelson deplored these restrictions on the future of scholarly archaeology but he did feel that for the present the Negev was a logical area for him to explore. Certainly his work there could have the most practical applications for the future of Israel.

To prove his theories about the Negev, Nelson was prepared to do what he had done in his Transjordan survey. Again he would walk through every square mile of the rocky desert, from Beersheba to Aqabah, and examine the land for traces of its history.

It was widely believed, in modern times, that the Negev had always been an empty wilderness. The common assumption was that climatic conditions over the ages had become so forbidding that neither man nor animal could exist there in domesticity. Only the desert Bedouins, wandering in pursuit of water for their flocks, had managed to survive in the Negev.

Nelson was troubled by this supposition. He knew of too many facts contradicting it.

He knew, for instance, that many ancient travel and trade routes had led through the Negev. If the Bible was to be believed, Abraham and his followers had journeyed through the Negev on their way from Canaan to Egypt. During the Exodus, the Israelites had spent many years wandering in the Negev.

Nelson himself had found proof that King Solomon used the Negev as his line of protection and communication between Ezion-geber and Jerusalem.

The Queen of Sheba, on her long trip to Solomon's

capital, must have rested and refreshed herself at way stations along the Negev route.

Other archaeologists had found the remains of churches, monasteries, even towns of the Roman and Byzantine times in the Negev, so certainly the wilderness had been inhabited during later periods of its history. The important question was, how had the desert dwellers sustained themselves? How had they gotten their food and water?

If, as Nelson believed, the Negev had been inhabited during various times—but never consecutively—what had brought about the disappearance of human settlements? Had the climate really changed so much that the desert became too dry and inhospitable for people to live there?

The Transjordan studies he had made would be of the greatest help in his Negev project, Nelson decided. He suspected that many things he had discovered in Transjordan would hold true in the Negev too. Both in location and in the nature of its terrain, Transjordan was much like the Negev-Sinai area. But, important as his previous findings might be, nothing he had done until now would have the great, direct value to the young Israelis seeking to colonize the desert as the work he hoped to do in the Negev now.

When, in 1952, Nelson began to explore the uncharted wilderness of the Negev, he took with him not only the good wishes of the new State of Israel. Part of its army went with him too.

Though the methods of archaeology had advanced in recent years, human nature had not. It was now less safe than ever for an adventurous explorer to search out the lands of the Bible! Arab snipers and terrorists made it impossible for him to travel alone.

**Dr. Nelson Glueck at the Wadi Arabah in Palestine (Israel) in
1942. Most desert exploration still had be done using camels for
transportation.**

Courtesy of the American Jewish Archives on the
Cincinnati Campus of the Hebrew Union College-Jewish Institute of Religion

After the birth of the State of Israel, Nelson Glueck was accompanied by soldiers on all his expeditions, traveling by jeep wherever he went.

On each field trip he was now joined by rifle-carrying soldiers who kept sharp watch on every ancient trail. Gone were the days when his hours of solitary investigation were shared by a lone guide. As many as fifteen to twenty men now composed his guard. Nelson had to learn to make the best of this new development.

In a land so filled with amateur archaeologists, Nelson found it easy to pick out young soldiers whose enthusiasm for reconstructing history matched his own. Their eagerness to be part of his team was inspiring.

The soldiers became students, and Nelson their teacher. Both he and they treasured those times when, huddled near protective craggy rocks, the group sat listening to him reading portions of the Bible. The selections he read always dealt with the region they were exploring. In the right setting this group of men even looked like figures out of the Exodus. Squatting on the ground in the soft shadows of a desert evening, they might have been some Israelites looking to their leader for a way out of the wilderness. And their leader, bronzed by the strong sun, wearing a Bedouin headdress against the wind and heat, might easily have passed as a tribal chieftain.

A penetrating glance at the group and its equipment quickly dispelled such romantic notions. Instead of camels, jeeps were parked nearby. Nelson and his military escort moved over the desert in jeeps, not only because they shortened travel time. Jeeps could carry the necessary rifles, grenades, and machine guns, and the field radio for summoning quick help.

Nelson had never really liked camels as a mode of transportation. Their stubbornness and disagreeable temper were not difficult to give up. But he did not like traveling with an armed camp either. He missed the almost personal style of his former explorations. It was so different when he could stroll through the land looking for clues, put down his sleeping bag wherever night overtook him, and have his guide bake pitta for their evening meal.

Crossing the Negev with a soldier guard of twenty demanded organization. Stops had to be planned and sufficient food brought along to feed everyone. Instead of an exploration, each field trip now became a full expedition.

There were unexpected rewards. Many times in later years Nelson had surprise reunions with some of the young men who had surveyed the desert with him. And he never denied the thrill of pleasure he felt each time someone—a taxi-driver in Jerusalem, a waiter in Tel-Aviv, or a pedestrian anywhere on a street in Israel—approached him with outstretched hand and said, "Shalom, Professor. Remember me? I was with you when you dug in the Negev."

"Our task was to spy out the Negev."

Nelson kept this ever in mind as he and the young men with him endured the cruel midday sun and the equally distressing cold of the desert nights. Often enough they thought of the Israelites and their complaints about the discomforts of this wilderness. Nelson read his companions passages about the Exodus, and all sympathized with the biblical desert wanderers, who longed for the green pastures and the abundant water supply they had left behind in Egypt. At least the explorers knew that their field trips would last only two weeks at a time.

It was their job to learn how ancient peoples had survived here. There were many ways of doing this; Nelson started with the land, its geography and its shape. This told him how roads were formed. Roads never disappeared; they were used by different civilizations throughout the centuries. Some of the trails used by modern Bedouins had carried traffic since the days of antiquity.

Soil and water told a story of their own. It was still a good archaeological bet that the location of a water source would lead to the discovery of signs of human settlement. Nelson pursued his hunt for water in the Negev, much as he had done in Transjordan, and he was not disappointed. Some of the remains of towns and villages he found near dried-up stream beds and springs dated back to 6000 B.C.E.

Nelson's most pleasant surprises in the Negev came every time he rediscovered traces left by the Nabataeans.

The Nabataeans were an Arab people of the pre-Christian period whose skills he had learned to know and appreciate during his years of surveying in Transjordan. There he had found their roads and cities and discovered that the Nabataeans must have had great building talents. Not much was known about them.

In 1937, at a site named Khirbet Tannur in the south of Transjordan, Nelson had excavated a small temple belonging to the Nabataeans and had become fascinated with their great artistic sense. With his writings on the breakthrough at Khirbet Tannur, Nelson helped to bring the accomplishments of the Nabataeans before the eyes of the general public for the first time.

Shortly before the start of the common era, the Nabataeans had left Transjordan and moved into the Negev. Here, in the 1950s, Nelson came upon their relics again and marveled at the way these people had adapted themselves to the dry, barren desert by inventing and building water systems that had kept them alive and their fields flourishing.

In the water-poor climate of the Negev, some areas receive as little as one or two inches of rain per year. When they come, the winter rains often pour down in torrents that last only a few minutes. The water does not sink into the ground, where it would fertilize the soil, but is caught in the rock-hard wadis, and these "rivers in the desert" foam and rush past the dry areas that need moisture so sorely.

To trap the desperately needed rainwater, the Nabataeans built dams which prevented the flashfloods from leaving the stream beds. This forced the water to sink into the ground instead of running out and left the soil in this spot fertile enough for cultivating.

Another favorite conservation system of the Nabataeans was to terrace their hilltops. Every drop of rainwater that fell on these heights was channeled to the growing fields of crops in the valley below.

When Nelson examined the Negev closely, he found thousands of huge cisterns carved deeply into rock. These were the storage cellars used by the Nabataeans to make certain of a water supply even during the bone-dry desert summers. With the aid of these gigantic subterranean storehouses they always had sufficient water for themselves and their animals, and for the strangers whose caravans traveled through their region.

Made watertight by the application of many layers of plaster, these cisterns were often still in excellent condition. It was of great amazement to Nelson that centuries of idleness had done little harm to their usefulness. His respect increased for the skill of the people who had carved these cisterns so diligently and well without the benefit of modern machinery and drills. With a little bit of cleaning and repair, twentieth-century desert dwellers would benefit from the labors of the Nabataeans so many hundreds of years before.

Technical advances made during World War II resulted in many new tools that archaeologists now found helpful. Perhaps the most useful new tool of the postwar era was Carbon 14. With its use archaeologists can now determine the age of many artifacts they unearth during their excavacations. Dating has become a precise science, instead of the guessing game it had long been. In the words of the *World Book Encyclopedia*, this is how Carbon 14 works:

> All living plants and animals, including man, take in radiocarbon from the air. This substance is radioactive, or gives off rays. After the living thing dies, the radiocarbon in its remains loses radioactivity at a fixed rate over thousands of years.
> . . . When a tree is cut down, it dies and stops taking in radiocarbon. But the radiocarbon in its wood goes on decaying at its constant rate. Perhaps wood from a certain tree was used in the coffin of an Egyptian king. We can measure the radiations from the radiocarbon left in the wood, and learn how old the wood is. This tells us about when the king died.

Nelson often felt that the rapid advance of scientific tools had come a little too late for him. Although he had no need for them in his Negev survey, he looked back on his past discoveries, especially his excavations at Khirbet Tannur and Ezion-geber, and he often wondered how much more he might have accomplished had these modern methods and tools been available to him at the time.

The Bible and the pottery code remained Nelson's principal means of identifying his discoveries. He never doubted that the "historical memory" of the Bible was his best guide. Nowhere was this as true as in the Negev, where fact and faith often intertwined.

The Negev is not like any other desert. Nelson did not even think of it as a true desert. He knew it had been inhabited at various times. He also knew that no other place on earth had played as important a role in the cross-fertilization of ideas. The region had been the setting for many well-

known Bible stories. It had closely influenced the lives of
Abraham and Moses.

In this "land of wide horizons and open spaces, where
divinity once made itself apparent," Nelson was seared by
the sun and swallowed pounds of wind-driven desert
dust. But he succeeded in searching out the Negev mile
by mile, and he found out many of its historical secrets.
He also became spellbound by the spirit of the great
personalities who had made this region their own. For
Nelson, exploring the Negev became a "going back to the
land of our belonging."

When he dug at the Negev site of Tell Abu Matar, he
found the skeleton of a newborn child buried under a
fireplace. Nearby, he and his companions discovered the
tiny remains of an infant imbedded in the foundation of a
housewall. At still another tell in the Negev, the scientists
unearthed the body of a baby, stuffed in a jar, buried
under a threshold.

Archaeologists had been finding such ghastly disclo-
sures all over the country, so it was immediately clear to
Nelson that he had discovered evidence of the hideous
cult of child sacrifice. Contemporary archaeologists believed that long before the counting of time, the firstborn
son of every family in these lands had been offered to the
gods in hopes of invoking favor upon the household.
Sacrificing their first child, whether by "passing it
through the fire" or by other means, was the accepted
price parents paid for a large future family, fertile flocks,
and fruitful fields. It was a rite that had existed, unques-
tioned, for hundreds of centuries.

Child sacrifice must have taken place in the Negev
during the time Abraham lived there. Nelson estimated
that time to have been during the nineteenth century
B.C.E. The ritual continued long after Abraham's day, but
an incident in the life of the Patriarch quietly signaled the
moment of change.

The Bible describes in detail the scene on Mount Moriah, to which the Lord had commanded Abraham to bring his favorite son, Isaac. The climax of the well-known story comes, of course, when Abraham, at the bidding of his God, substitutes a ram for the expected human sacrifice.

A gentle revolution had its start at this moment of Abraham's refusal to participate in the sacrificial worship of his time. By shattering superstition Abraham brought about a change of everlasting importance.

Never again would the people of Abraham be like the neighboring tribes in the desert. While all around them others prayed to many gods, Abraham and his followers worshipped the One God who had commanded them to save a human life and serve Him in righteousness. This would be the core of their religion forever after.

Summing up his Negev experiences in the popular book *Rivers in the Desert*, Nelson gave the poetic title "Heartland of Conscience" to his chapter on the area. Describing the Negev and the adjacent wilderness of Sinai, he points out that they had been the sites of Israel's most important religious experiences. From there "the dawning of conscience" had spread, being taken up by Jesus and his disciples and by the followers of Mohammed. Despite all the setbacks throughout the ages, nothing, Nelson felt, had influenced mankind as much as the "still, small voice" first heard in the wilderness of the Holy Land.

It was perhaps not strange that God had revealed His will to Abraham in the Negev and to Moses on Mount Sinai, away from the distractions of cities and crowds. The solitude of the desert was a most auspicious setting for the God of Israel to make His voice heard for all time.

During the untold number of field trips Nelson made out of his headquarters at Sde Boker in the 1950s, he located

more than five hundred ancient sites and wells in the
Negev area between Beersheba and Eilat. Many of these
sites he linked positively to the Age of Abraham through
potsherds. He was especially excited to find that these
pottery fragments were of one distinct type. Both its
greenish-gray color and the envelope or ear-shape of its
handles made this pottery easy to recognize. Because
Nelson discovered that no settled human life had existed
in the Negev—and in Transjordan—before and after the
nineteenth century B.C.E., he concluded that the unique
earthenware he found throughout both areas must have
belonged to the time in which he placed Abraham.

Finding the pottery so widely spread near the un-
fortified clusters of round stone houses beside wells and
cisterns in the desert, Nelson was convinced that the Age
of Abraham had been a time of general peace and
prosperity. His archaeological discoveries and the Bible
told him this must have been a time for travel and trade
over the caravan arteries that led through the Negev and
connected its neighbors to the east and west.

At different times in history, people had lived off this
dry land, using all their skill and knowledge to trap and
utilize the precious rainfall. Their very existence here
proved that the Negev had never been a total wasteland.
The Judaeans, and after them the Nabataeans, had tamed
the Negev sufficiently to raise fields of barley, grain, and
lentils. Their herds of sheep and goats had grazed at the
edges of these farming communities, which were walled
in to conserve every drop of moisture in the soil.

Even before he began his Negev explorations, Nelson
suspected that the Negev had always been fruitful. He
had shared Prime Minister Ben-Gurion's belief that the
southland had once been inhabited. Now Nelson's con-
clusions made him very hopeful for this large section of
Israel, still unused and unexploited. Surely the energetic,

resourceful Israelis would find a way to make the desert fertile once more.

Frequently during his desert excursions Nelson asked himself why there had never been a continuous chain of habitation in the Negev. Why had periods of human occupation here alternated with long stretches of emptiness? He had asked the same question while working in Transjordan, for there, too, civilizations had come and gone in a similar pattern.

In apparent harmony with their natural habitat, people had come into both areas to live, grow, and develop a civilization. Then, after a few generations, all life would stop. Suddenly, abruptly, the civilization disappeared. The desert was silent for another spell of timelessness. Only the moan of the wind was heard in the open vastness—and in time the footfalls of the nomadic Bedouins, as they returned to reclaim the land.

In the Book of Genesis Nelson found the story of the mighty king Chedorlaomer, most bloodthirsty of the "Kings of the East." Certainly it was not the first time he had studied the biblical account of Chedorlaomer, whose campaign of wanton destruction was so great and horrifying that generations preserved his evil deeds, passing them on as a warning to their children until almost one thousand years after the event it was recorded by scribes of the Bible.

Avenging the rebellion of several minor kings against him, King Chedorlaomer's troops had killed, plundered, and scorched the earth in city after city, from Syria southward into Sinai. When Nelson compared the sites in which he had found wrecked and ruined remains of houses, fields, and whole villages with the list of place-names in the Bible, he found to his complete amazement that most of them matched. No scholar before him had accepted this biblical story as anything but a legend. Now Nelson found archaeological evidence to back up his theory: not time had wrecked and ruined the places he had examined, but an ancient invader whose urge to destroy had been overwhelming in its intensity.

The peaceful Age of Abraham had been put to an end by the warring hordes of Chedorlaomer. Nelson found the evidence for this in the now-familiar pottery of the time of Abraham at sites which clearly bore the marks of violent destruction. The story of King Chedorlaomer's assault and destruction was only one chapter in the history of the Negev. Nelson suspected that other civilizations at various times had suffered a similar fate at the hands of fierce invaders. He had found what he was looking for.

He was now certain that those who claimed that changes of climate over the centuries had made the Negev uninhabitable did not know the true facts. Nothing Nelson had discovered in the geography of Israel's southland convinced him that the Negev or the Transjordan territory had undergone any significant weather changes in the last ten thousand years. Warfare and human violence had been to blame for the disappearance of whole civilizations that had tried to live in the Negev. And that was an old story which had little to do with the weather.

Today there is a postscript to all the exploring, soil sampling, and mapping of archaeologists like Nelson Glueck and others in the Negev. Their stubborn obsession to bring this uncharted wilderness to life again was only the first step. Others have taken up the challenge.

Today the ancient international trade routes are in use again. The roads that run through the Negev are paved and heavily traveled. The donkeys and camels of those vital caravan lanes have been replaced by trucks and jeeps carrying Israel's most important minerals to the modern harbors of Eilat and Ashdod. From there goods are shipped to the Far East for millions of dollars in trade payments.

Potash, nitrate, and phosphate, mined in the immediate vicinity of the Dead Sea, mean big business to Israel. The fertilizers produced from these minerals help Israel grow its own food, while the surplus is sold to foreign countries. Hundreds of workers and their families, attracted to the Negev because of its job opportunities, now live in the chain of new cities built to house them.

Arad, Dimona, and Eilat are the new cities in the desert that were founded in the 1950s. Beersheba, at whose wells Abraham watered his flocks, is now the official capital of the Negev, with a university of its own. Surrounding the cities of the Negev are over thirty communal farms, producing such important crops as sugar beets, cotton, peanuts, and out-of-season vegetables.

Daily El Al, the Israeli airline, flies a top-priority cargo to Europe: flowers and vegetables grown in the Wadi Arabah. Melons and tomatoes are sold for high prices in the capitals of Europe during the winter season. High-stemmed gladiolus raised in the hot-house climate of the Wadi Arabah are among the most expensive blooms in European flower shops at Christmastime.

In the many years of his work Nelson had foreseen that some of these accomplishments were possible, and, of course, he was enormously pleased with the practical results his archaeological discoveries had produced in the Negev. He had always believed a great lesson could be learned from the accomplishments of long-ago generations who had tried to tame the desert. And now the Israelis have proved him right.

13

It had happened right after the new State of Israel was created, during Nelson's first trip back to Jerusalem.

As he settled down in his hotel room, he made plans for the next day. One of the first places he would visit would be the American School on Saladin Road. This was a routine he had followed for years each time he arrived in the city.

When he set out for his old headquarters the next morning, an unpleasant discovery awaited him.

"You can't get across here, sir. This is the border," an armed young Israeli soldier informed Nelson when he reached the barbed-wire fence separating one side of a street from the other. "Unless you have a government pass, I cannot let you through."

Nelson stared through the mesh of the fence. On the other side a Jordanian soldier with a rifle stared back.

Only about a mile from here he could see the flat roof of the American School. To think that for so many years he had been director of the school and now it was suddenly off-limits to him!

It seemed like a bad dream. Nelson walked back to his hotel, thinking he would call the school from there and tell his colleagues he could not get over to them for his planned visit. In his best Hebrew he told the operator he wished to talk to the American School on Saladin Road.

"Sorry, sir. We have no connection between Jerusalem, Israel, and Jerusalem, Jordan. There is no way I can complete your call."

This was incredible. Just last night, after his arrival, he had talked to New York and gotten his call through within a few minutes. But here he was, one mile away from the building he knew so well, and he could not contact anyone either in person or by telephone.

For decades the American School had served as a clearinghouse of information for all American scholars interested in the archaeology of the Near East. But now, because of its location in East Jerusalem, which belonged to Jordan, the use of the school was restricted to those scholars and students who happened to live in the Jordanian part of Jerusalem. No longer could Nelson visit the laboratory where he had begun his intense study of the pottery code which had unlocked so much of the past for him.

Of course, Nelson was not the only person to whom the school was out of bounds. The restriction applied to all Israeli archaeologists and any foreign scholars who lived in the Israeli part of Jerusalem. For them there was now no place to deposit new information, no headquarters where discoveries could be shared with other English-speaking colleagues, no school where young ar-chaeologists could train to go out researching the biblical past.

It was a hateful situation. No one deplored these artificial barriers more than Nelson, who believed that the interchange of ideas was vitally important to human cultural progress.

"It is a pity," he wrote, "that one cannot live for a thousand years or two, because in the course of time the silly man-made borders are expunged by the erosion of time and by the compulsions of geopolitics."

He had his own reasons for resenting these "man-made borders." The eastern part of the Wadi Arabah and Tell el-Kheleifeh, all the territory in which Nelson had worked, lay on "the other side of the Jordan." All these areas were inaccessible to him now. And he had always wanted to go back to them for more work.

He was certain that an ancient Solomonic fortress lay hidden on the heights overlooking the Wadi Arabah, and he wanted to investigate it. That land now belonged to Jordan.

He had always hoped to excavate further at Tell el-Kheleifeh, but that mound lay in the no-man's land between Israel and Jordan, and he was not allowed there.

He did not complain publicly. Most Israelis had sacrificed far more in the War of Independence. But he would never be able to return to the places where he had done his most intense, most creative work. And that hurt deeply.

For many years Nelson dreamed that Hebrew Union College might one day have a branch in Jerusalem, the heartland of Judaism. His dream had its start early during his presidency of the College, even before he announced his hope that every rabbinical student would be able to spend his first year of studies in Israel.

The dream was brought back to Nelson by the closing of the border between the two Jerusalems. The time had come to listen to the practical side of his personality, and that said, "Do it now."

When the doors of his former workshop were closed to him, Nelson recognized the need to replace the services the American School of Oriental Research had offered before. Israeli Jerusalem needed a school of its own for the advanced study of archaeology and biblical subjects.

To Nelson, having such a school built under the auspices of the Hebrew Union College–Jewish Institute of Religion seemed a perfect solution. Since the College-Institute was already awarding degrees to graduate students from all over America who attended classes on the Cincinnati campus, a postgraduate center in Jerusalem would be a natural extension. If he could interest other American institutions in becoming a part of this new school, sharing its facilities, another one of his greatest hopes would be realized. American scholars of all denominations would be able to consider the Jerusalem School their research home in the Holy Land.

In America all the branches of the College-Institute were centers for the training of rabbis and religious leaders. It would be different at the Jerusalem branch. Here the main emphasis would be on the study of Bible and archaeology in an American-sponsored setting.

But the religious influence would be there. Not for a moment did Nelson forget that he wanted a school which would represent the spirit of liberal Judaism. He planned a chapel for it which would be an important part of the school. The chapel would be the site of Sabbath services, and each Jewish holy day would be celebrated in it according to the ritual of American Reform. At last, American rabbinical students spending a year in Israel would have a spiritual headquarters to call their own.

Nelson knew very well that no part of his plan would stir up as much trouble in Israel as the building of the chapel. Israel did not have separation of state and religion. It was under the strict rule of the Orthodox rabbinate, which guarded its power jealously. The very last thing such an establishment wanted was a liberal house of prayer built right under their noses.

But he was also determined. When reporters from the evening newspaper *Ma'ariv* interviewed him, he stated publicly that he hoped all Jews in Israel would be entitled to religious freedom.

It was time to find out whether his dream could become

reality. And the first step was to convince his Israeli friends to help him.

Nelson's love affair with Israel was not one-sided. It was a very special, personal connection on both sides.

In Israel he was known as "The Professor," not as Dr. Glueck or Rabbi Glueck. The city of Eilat made him an honorary citizen as a reward for his discoveries there. Beersheba, the heart of the Negev, also conferred honorary citizenship upon Nelson after his desert explorations were done.

Private citizens and important cabinet members alike shared his friendship and respected the unpretentious American who had established a firm link between Israel's historic past and her urgent present.

Among his friends Nelson counted David Ben-Gurion, with whom he walked in the desert and discussed the future of the Negev. Golda Meir prepared him tea in her own kitchen and then sat listening to his ideas on the separation of religion and politics in Israel.

Nelson was just as much at home with the Jerusalem taxi-driver who refused payment from him when he recognized his passenger as the discoverer of King Solomon's Mines. Or with the Tel-Aviv waiter who reserved his best table for the man who had excavated legendary Ezion-geber.

It was an open secret that Nelson enjoyed a special status among Israelis. They had shared with him the happy excitement of his archaeological discoveries right in their own country. And they liked him because he proved by his theories what they had for so long tried to explain to the rest of the world: the Jewish people had always belonged to the land of the Bible.

Nelson was far too modest to expect personal privileges from his friendship with prominent Israeli leaders. But he did not hesitate when it came to talking about his projected school. Then he talked to everyone who might be able to help. And he was heard.

In 1955 Nelson came home to the United States carrying with him an important bit of news. For once even El Al's fastest plane seemed slow and the stopover in New York longer than he cared to stay. Not until he was back in Cincinnati, facing his Board of Governors, did he trust himself to reveal the information he had brought them.

When he looked at the amazement in their eyes, and the joy, he knew for certain that his dream was on its way to reality. For the news he had brought them was that the Israeli government, under the leadership of Prime Minister Moshe Sharett, had granted to the College-Institute a free, perpetual lease to two acres of land right in the heart of Jerusalem.

Two acres on King David Street, close to the Pontifical Library and the French Embassy, just a few steps away from the Jerusalem YMCA and the landmark of the King David Hotel—on this, the most desirable property in the city, their school would be built.

Nelson glowed as he described to them the priceless location where he had stood and looked over to the Old City. Future generations of students coming to Jerusalem to study the past would stand where he had stood, he said, and they would sense history by merely gazing across the Valley of Hinnom toward the ancient walls girdling the Old City.

If they closed their eyes and followed Nelson's words, they could picture the finished school as it would one day rise from this slope off King David Street. All that was left to do was to go out and raise the money . . .

All he had to do was to raise the money. He had the consent of the Board of Governors and their enthusiastic pledge of support. But he would have to find some private donors. Suddenly the enormous task ahead of him hit Nelson.

It was some job he had chosen for himself. And for a man without the talent for making money he was certainly cast in the wrong role.

He knew first-hand the many urgent projects that demanded assistance in Israel. Housing, roads, social services . . . they all needed money—money that came from America. Generous Americans were eager and anxious to help with the building of those houses and roads. They would contribute toward settling and feeding the newcomers to Israel. But would there be any money left for building his school?

Nelson felt an intense urge to build that center in Jerusalem. Like his famous predecessor, Isaac Mayer Wise, founder of the American Jewish Reform movement, Nelson knew he could enlist the cooperation of others to achieve his goals. He firmly believed in his own powers of persuasion. He would convince enough backers that the school he had in mind would perform a service. It would be the headquarters for a common effort, an ecumenical effort composed of many elements. Tolerant of each other, scholars, both secular and religious, would study man's historical background and make scientific discoveries, proving at the same time that people of good will can work together.

He really did not mind seeking out donors, even if it took trips all over the United States. Of course, it meant spending even less time with Helen, who was now a hardworking full professor of medicine at the University Medical School in Cincinnati. And he would hardly see Charlie, his son, who was setting records as an outstanding student at Harvard.

Nelson took a little notebook from his pocket. In it he jotted down names—the names of people who might want

to help him build the Jerusalem School. He made a list of
the cities he would need to visit. Like a politician on a
barnstorming mission—or an archaeologist preparing an
expedition of major importance—he carefully laid out his
plan. The campaign was on!

In April 1958, after six seasons of work in the Negev,
Nelson returned to New York and called a press confer-
ence.

Some of the reporters who came to the West 68th
Street office of Hebrew Union College–Jewish Institute of
Religion had never seen Nelson Glueck in person before.
Except for his deep suntan, the lean man on the podium,
dressed in a dark business suit and tie, hardly fitted their
conception of an explorer who braved the wilds of the
desert. But they had all seen photographs of Nelson
Glueck at work in the desert, and they felt they knew him
far better dressed in the open-shirted khaki uniform he
wore when ranging through the hot, dry Negev.

He had called them, Nelson said, because during his
latest search in the Negev his expedition had located a
150-mile stretch of the ancient Way of Shur.

It was an exciting discovery. Three separate books of
the Bible mentioned the Way of Shur, but until now it had
never been fixed to an exact location.

The road had been used frequently by Abraham. Isaac
and Jacob, too, had journeyed on it. But, most im-
portantly, it was mentioned in Exodus as the road on
which the Israelites, led by Moses, trudged wearily after
leaving Egypt.

Nelson reported how his group had discovered the Way
of Shur.

Not far from Beersheba, which had always been a vital
trade center throughout the history of the Near East,
Nelson and his expedition had found several tracks that

led to one broader road which looked very old to them. Moving from Beersheba westward into the Sinai desert, the Glueck group had followed the road as far as the Egyptian border.

Along the way they had found the remains of two ancient Judaean fortresses that must have once guarded the highway. This they took as a sign that the road had been an important trade route between the Judaean kingdom and Egypt.

From the fortress ruins and the remains of nearby stone houses, Nelson retrieved a plentiful sampling of pottery fragments. There were enough potsherds to make a definite identification.

Once again the "magic window" allowed them an amazingly accurate glimpse into the distant past. For Nelson and his men there was little doubt: they were standing on a section of the Way of Shur described by the Bible.

"We reasoned that if we could find the road traveled by Abraham from Canaan to Egypt, and back again," Nelson explained, "we would be on the same road traveled by the Israelites."

It was only another year before Nelson could announce— in 1959—finding another important Negev route, this one in use for at least five thousand years.

Nelson's team, using its Beersheba headquarters, had again been searching the Negev for ancient village sites when, about thirty-five miles to the south of Kibbutz Sde Boker, it had come across an old trail known in the area as Darb-es-Sultani (Road of the Sultan).

At first Nelson believed this road to be of local importance only. But then he remembered that such names as the Sultan's Road or the Royal Road were usually given to a route because of a tradition based on fact.

He examined the Darb-es-Sultani closer and found that it ran eastward as far as the present Jordanian border. There it connected with the ancient King's Highway. And the King's Highway was definitely linked to the story of the Israelites during the Exodus.

Usually the discovery of an age-old caravan route only interests other archaeologists, or historians who can reconstruct a whole series of civilizations around such a find. This was not the case with Nelson's identification of the Way of Shur.

Every year during their Passover festival, Jewish people all over the world recall the time when their forefathers left the slavery of Egypt behind in their search for the Promised Land. For centuries Jews had read in their Haggadahs the story of the Israelites and their forty years of wandering in the wilderness. Now the modern science of archaeology confirmed part of the story to be absolutely true. The road on which their ancestors had trekked to freedom had been discovered.

Nelson encountered the spirit of history often while exploring the Negev. But one particular experience remained in his memory.

It took place during a camp-out near Beersheba at the time of Rosh Hashanah. When the holy day approached Nelson gave his assistants a choice. They could spend the day in the town of Beersheba or stay in camp. The unanimous decision was to stay in the desert.

"We traded some canned rations to the Arabs for a young goat, which we dressed and prepared for the feast. Reading from a Reform prayer book, I conducted the services overlooking the ancient Biblical site . . ."

Encamped in the sands of the Negev, Nelson and the young men with him began yet another new year of the ancient Hebrew calendar. For Nelson and his team—

most of them Israelis—past and present fused that night in the spirit of timelessness that engulfed them in the wilderness.

Their thoughts were of the men who long ago might have watched the same stars rise in the tranquil autumn sky. Perhaps it was on this very spot that their ancestors had sat and wondered what the new year might have in store for them.

The long chain of time that tied the present generation to their forefathers shrank into an invisible link that evening. Neither Nelson nor his companions soon forgot the Rosh Hashanah they had celebrated in the desert.

14

On a wintry day in early January of 1961, millions of television viewers all over the world saw John F. Kennedy sworn in as President of the United States. Hopes ran high in Washington that day that a new era in government was about to begin—an era of cultural and scientific excitement in which the young President would lead his country to fresh new heights of achievement. The many important people in the arts and sciences who had been invited to the inaugural ceremony signified the new times that lay ahead.

The President-to-be had asked his favorite poet, Robert Frost, to participate in the ceremonial by reading one of his works. He had also requested another man he admired highly to say the closing prayer.

When the time came for the final benediction, a tall, straight man on the podium stepped in front of ex-Presidents and cabinet officers and spoke into the microphone, which carried his voice to all corners of the earth.

"May the Lord bless thee and keep thee," he intoned in Hebrew, and raised his arms wide in priestly blessing.

"May the Lord make His face to shine upon thee, and be gracious unto thee," pronounced the rabbi in velvet-trimmed black robes.

"May the Lord lift up His countenance, and give thee peace."

With these ancient words of sanctification, Nelson

Glueck, head of Hebrew Union College–Jewish Institute of Religion, launched the "New Frontier" of the Kennedy administration.

Nelson Glueck? Many who knew the name didn't know he was a rabbi. The general public mainly remembered him as the explorer who had opened an old, new world to their view. For Nelson Glueck was the man responsible for a curious phenomenon that had occurred in the English-speaking world shortly after 1959.

Many a person who until then had known nothing about biblical archaeology now began mentioning place-names like Eilat, Timna, or the Wadi Arabah in conversations. The topic of King Solomon's Mines became a favorite at the dinner tables of people who had never set foot in the Near East. Art fanciers who knew little about Semitic civilizations started collecting pottery excavated in the Holy Land.

Behind this sudden and strong interest in the Near East and its archaeology was the appearance of the book *Rivers in the Desert*, which Nelson wrote after finishing his work in the Negev.

It was not the usual scientific presentation an interested reader might find in an archaeological journal. This was a trip into the historical past, absolutely real—and believable. Nelson had made it so with his vivid storytelling.

He described fortresses in the Negev which had once guarded important highways, and even an armchair traveler could see the messengers of the kings of Judah shuttling between Jerusalem and Eilat.

He pictured ancient caravansaries in the desert that conjured up visions of travelers as important as the Queen of Sheba and her retinue halting there for overnight stops.

He narrated facts about idol worship and child sacrifice that made it easy to believe in Abraham and Moses as

Rabbi Nelson Glueck delivering the Benediction at the inauguration of President John F. Kennedy in Washington, D.C., January 20, 1961.

Courtesy of the American Jewish Archives on the
Cincinnati Campus of the Hebrew Union College–Jewish Institute of Religion

**Nelson and Helen Glueck at the dedication of the Jerusalem School
of the Hebrew Union College, March 29, 1963.**

living persons who were influenced by their natural and cultural surroundings into starting new customs of religion and morality.

As Nelson traced the threads of history through his discoveries, he added his own emotional and religious feelings to the descriptions. This made his writing different from any other that had appeared on the subject of biblical research. It also gave it popular appeal.

He had never intended any of his scientific work to "prove" the accuracy of the Bible but then found that most of his archaeological discoveries bore out the amazing literal truth in the Bible.

Because of Nelson's talent to paint with the pen, he was able to reveal a true, new picture of the wilderness of the Negev. It was a picture few people would ever see for themselves.

"It is a land of sharp contrasts," he wrote,

of surprising fertility and extreme barrenness, of delicate flowers and fierce bushes armed with tearing spikes, of rain in scarcity and cisterns without number, of extreme dryness and heavy dew. It is a land of great heat by day and bitter cold by night, of some amazing riches and much unrelieved poverty, of cultivable plains, high and broken plateaus, deep canyons, and innumerable dry stream beds that on rare occasions are hosts to short-lived torrents. It is a strong land of wide horizons and open spaces where divinity once made itself apparent and where sturdy pioneers seek once again to strike root.

"Government and Jewish Agency members are vying with each other to do honor to this newest venture in

Jerusalem for scholarship and religion," wrote a newspaper reporter when Hebrew Union College's School of Archaeology was inaugurated in July 1963.

Prime Minister Ben-Gurion, Abba Eban, Moshe Sharett, Golda Meir, the President of Israel, Yitzhak Ben-Zvi, and many others took part in a round of festive activities during which the Jerusalem School's modern main building, sleek and straight in its sheath of white Galilee limestone, was opened.

Among many highlights of that happy July weekend, one was of special pleasure to Nelson. During the opening convocation, at which Prime Minister Ben-Gurion spoke, honorary degrees were presented to two persons particularly dear to Nelson. The Jerusalem School conferred its first honorary Doctorate of Hebrew Letters upon Yigal Yadin, famous for his excavation of Masada, and Nelson's fellow student at Dr. Albright's school. A Doctorate of Humane Letters went to Professor Carl W. Blegen, chairman of the classics department of the University of Cincinnati and internationally known for his excavation of Troy.

The weekend of convocations, receptions, and dinners began with a Friday night religious service in the William Murstein Synagogue, the very same chapel which had been the biggest obstacle to the building of the school.

Two hundred and twenty-five guests filled every seat of the impressive sanctuary, with its white marble Ark covered by a handwoven green curtain, and a floor-to-ceiling sweep of tall windows whose light bathed the synagogue in a soft, ethereal glow.

Nelson's deep, dark eyes brimmed as he looked around at the many friends who had come to join him in this special hour. Among them he recognized many a staunch ally who had willingly put his political career into danger by speaking out publicly in favor of granting this choice land to Hebrew Union College.

For Moshe Sharett's leasing agreement had come under fire and had to be defended in the Knesset, where debate broke out over it. Members of the Orthodox religious parties had uttered strong opinions against giving the land to the American Reform movement, but the Prime Minister had declared that under the Israeli constitution freedom was guaranteed to all religions.

When the Municipality of Jerusalem had rejected architectural plans for the school because they included sketches for a chapel, Mayor Gershon Agron had intervened on behalf of his friend Nelson Glueck. Mayor Agron never visited a synagogue himself, but in the interest of religious liberty he had insisted that this particular chapel must be built.

Of course, neither the mayor's permission nor the close friendship of Teddy Kollek could end the deep feelings of hostility against non-Orthodox Jews that still burned in Jerusalem.

For a moment Nelson's relaxed smile faded. He remembered the shot fired at him on this very spot while the foundations for the building were being laid and he was watching the workmen amid heaps of wooden boards, bricks, and beams. If ever the person firing at him had been caught by the local police, no one had told Nelson about it. It was one of those episodes everyone preferred to forget.

"I am not a brave man. I hate to be shot at," Nelson once said in a newspaper interview, years before. Then it was in answer to a question about the Arab nomads who had resented his appearance at their water hole in the Negev. Fearing he would seize their water, they had fired their rifles at him and his companions. But Nelson had pacified the Arabs, telling them he had no need for their well, but only wanted to investigate the land for scientific purposes.

That was not the only time Nelson had been the target

of gunmen. At the height of the Arab riots in the late thirties, a close friend had left Nelson's house and been shot dead in the street. Possibly the bullets had been intended for Nelson.

Daily, during that dangerous time, he had to commute to Jericho, where he continued his work on the Transjordan survey. Often he ducked bullets to get to his destination, but they never stopped him from going.

It was far more difficult to accept the hatred of fellow Jews who were fanatic enough to murder. Nelson kept out of certain sections of Jerusalem where he knew bodily harm might come to him. But he was angry to see intolerance perpetuated by religious power in the government. This, he felt, must be fought—on a higher level, of course. He looked forward to the day when both the Conservative and Reform branches of Judaism might take their challenge to court and test the power of the religious parties. Perhaps then all ordained rabbis—not only the Orthodox—would be allowed to function fully in Israel.

It sounded sweet to the ear to have the melodic strains of Oriental music weave through the service. Nelson had personally selected the music from among the treasures of the Sephardic liturgy. He hoped it would always be a part of the religious service in this sanctuary. He had reached far back for these wonderful Oriental tonalities, and he thought they would mingle well with the liberal ritual of Western Judaism. It would be a blending of the old and the new, just like this beautiful new school, which had risen on this hilly street in Jerusalem.

No organ was built into this chapel. The men and women sitting together to worship in the all-Hebrew service here were inspired by sounds that might have been heard within the walls of King Solomon's Temple, "a joyful noise" made by the human voice, woodwinds, and stringed instruments.

Nelson's face glowed. The clear, silvery sounds of the flute, the warm, velvety tune of the cello accompanied the words sung by the cantor and the female choir. And the words found their echo in Nelson's heart. "Let everything that hath breath praise the Lord. Hallelujah."

He was needed at home.

Unrest and despair followed the assassination of John F. Kennedy, hitting hardest at the young, whose hopes for bright, new leadership were cruelly cut down in Dallas. Violent confrontations on college campuses became the expression of students who, like university students throughout the ages, believed they could change the world for the better.

Unrest also touched the campus of the College-Institute in Cincinnati. Stirred by the plight of young blacks in the slum areas of the city, who had been battling police during several days of summer rioting, a group of rabbinical students felt moved to display their sense of solidarity with the underprivileged. They decided to march into downtown Cincinnati, carrying lighted candles as symbols of freedom, to demonstrate on behalf of their black brothers.

Nelson happened to be in Cincinnati on the evening of the proposed march. Some sort of sixth sense made him return to the campus long after the dinner hour, a time when all was usually quiet for the night.

Seeing the tense faces, the little knots of students, the candles, he sized up the situation at once. He called for an assembly on the lawn in front of the main building, to begin at once.

As head of the college Nelson was determined to prevent his students from an involvement in the local disorders. He saw no possible good in their planned demonstration. On the contrary, it was against his instincts to have these rabbinical students take part in a procession that would not only be fruitless but might bring injury to some of the young men. Their good intentions, he felt, were somewhat misdirected.

Nelson faced the crowd of young men, who were eager to be on their way but a little afraid to show disrespect to their president. He did not tell them they could not march downtown. Instead, he asked them to gather around him and sit down on the lawn. Hesitantly, uncertain, most of the students sat down, still holding their candles.

Nelson, the storyteller, took over. He talked to them. He spoke to them of his adventures, he described excavations he had directed. He exercised his special charm on them.

One by one the lighted candles went out. No one dared to move from the concentration of that gaze, which even in the dark hypnotized them. And Nelson talked on.

It was long after midnight that he stopped and looked around. He saw weary faces and limp, meek bodies, damp from sitting in the grass.

"Gentlemen," said the president of Hebrew Union College, "I hadn't realized it was so late. I guess we'd better call it a day."

15

Much kept Nelson busy during the mid-1960s. To his family and close friends, his vitality and energy were amazing. After all, they were *his* mid-sixties too. Still handsome and straight, he continued to spend three months out of every year in Israel doing archaeological work, showing up much younger men with his drive and endurance even during the hottest hours of the day.

Some of his zest for work had been transmitted to his son. Charles graduated from medical school with high honors and a record that gave promise of a brilliant career. Nelson was very proud of his son. He was pleased, too, that Helen's family had their fourth-generation physician.

Helen herself was now in charge of the coagulation laboratory at the University of Cincinnati, and her work, the study of blood clotting, was of great importance. Her professional feats had already become the background for a funny little story that made the rounds among family friends.

Late one afternoon the doorbell rang at 162 Glenmary Avenue. Nelson, who was home alone, answered the front door. Outside a young man asked to see Dr. Glueck.

"I am Dr. Glueck," said Nelson.

"No," insisted the caller, "I want to speak to the *real* Dr. Glueck."

Nelson had always wanted to write about the Nabataeans. Ever since he had excavated the Nabataean temple at Khirbet Tannur in Transjordan in 1937, he had felt a personal sense of discovery about this early people.

The Nabataeans continued to fascinate Nelson when he found, long after exploring Transjordan, that they had done such creative, lasting work with water conservation in the Negev. Although their civilization lasted only four centuries, these industrious people had left a permanent imprint on the land of Palestine.

Until the time when Nelson excavated their hilltop temple, the background of the Nabataeans had been veiled in mystery. Although Khirbet Tannur remained the only religious shrine of the Nabataeans to be uncovered, Nelson managed to clear up something of their culture and religion in his book *Deities and Dolphins*, which appeared in 1964.

Nelson considered it one of his major accomplishments to have solved the riddle of the dolphin symbol in Nabataean art. For years he had wondered why the Nabataeans should use dolphins as religious ornaments since they had been a landlocked people of the Arabian desert with no ties to the sea.

From his fascination with the Nabataeans grew much knowledge about them, which was later substantiated when other scholars discovered more evidence. The Nabataeans were a highly industrious, artistic people who were responsible for much of the drug and spice trade in the area of the Negev and Transjordania over which they ruled during the second and third centuries B.C.E. In their active and widespread trading they came into contact with the Greek culture, among others, and from it adopted a symbol sacred to the seafaring Greeks. The dolphin was considered a deity by the Greeks, who worshipped it as a symbol of their god Apollo. At the peak of their commercial success, the Nabataeans developed a high degree of artistic expression. It was during this time that they established religious sanctuaries along their trade routes in the desert. One of the figures appearing repeatedly in the decoration of their shrines was that of the dolphin.

Nelson was able to convince several Cincinnatians to purchase important pieces from the Khirbet Tannur excavation which he had shipped home years before. These were donated to the Cincinnati Art Museum and put on permanent view.

In a room filled with Nabataean statuary and sculpture, museum visitors may now gaze at remnants of the sanctuary which once stood on a solitary Jordanian mountaintop and served as a place of worship for the pilgrims who traveled the nearby spice and incense route from Arabia to Damascus.

Hebrew Union College Biblical and Archaeological School began its first excavation during the school year of 1964–65.

At a site near Gezer, once a major biblical city, the excavation was conducted, much like the earlier projects of the American School, by professors, students, and volunteers. The project at Gezer was to be an ongoing study which would last a number of years.

Although Tell Gezer was being excavated under the direction of Dr. William G. Dever of the Jerusalem School's staff, Nelson helped to launch the work. He supervised much of the training stage and coordinated it with Professor G. Ernest Wright of Harvard University, an old friend and colleague, whose group had joined the College-Institute as sponsors of the Gezer dig.

Already in its fledgling years the Jerusalem School was living up to Nelson's expectations. His dream for a consortium—that is, a group of outside universities and colleges that would take part in the school's operations—had come true.

Twenty-seven member institutions were already affiliated with this branch of the College-Institute, among them some of the leading schools in America. With the Gezer dig on its way and so many distinguished scholars associated with the Jerusalem School, the future looked bright for the operations at 13 King David Street.

On Monday, June 5, 1967, Israel went to war. Six days later three of Israel's neighbors, heavily armed and superior in numbers, had been defeated and the war was over.

At the end of that week, on Sunday, June 11, Nelson was on the El Al flight to Israel. He had been very worried about Israel's fate. As one of the first people to return to the victorious nation after the lightning-fast war, he was told many stories of the bravery displayed by Israelis during the fighting. Above all, he was impressed with the spirit of thanksgiving all Israelis had over their speedy and miraculous victory. Nelson kept a diary of his observations and feelings during this trip. The diary was later printed and published under the the the title *Dateline: Jerusalem.*

His immediate concern was for the Biblical and Archaeological School and how much damage it might have received during the shelling of Jerusalem. He was relieved to find that this was minor.

One of Nelson's first acts was to order the Gezer excavations to resume. The Summer Institute had been interrupted by the outbreak of the war. Many of the professional people connected with it were still in Israel, others had taken their families to Europe for safety. But all shared Nelson's feeling that there should be "business as usual" at the school.

When, six weeks later, the Summer Institute session came to an end, Nelson felt extremely proud of the high caliber and attractiveness of the young men who had taken part in this archaeological venture during a time of crisis.

Feeding Nelson's hopes for the continuing growth of the Jerusalem School was the gift of a new building, under construction despite the war. A close friend and admirer, Mrs. Rosaline Feinstein of Philadelphia, had given the funds for it and wanted it named in honor of Nelson. Today, however, the structure is known as the Feinstein Building.

Nelson felt positive about Israel's future, providing that direct negotiations between Israel and the hostile Arab countries could be arranged. Given the same spirit and purpose which he saw in Israel after the Six-Day War, Nelson felt a great sense of hope for peaceful conditions, stability, and economic and cultural advances in the Middle East.

Nelson hated to leave Jerusalem that fall. As always, saying goodbye to Jerusalem left an ache in his heart. With every departure he thought about how nice it would be to stay here for good. Plans for retirement always brought on visions of life in an apartment in Jerusalem, with Helen near him and archaeological sites close enough for quick visits.

Lately he had been wondering out loud how much more he might have accomplished had modern means been available to him at the time of his most important archaeological work. Helen assured him that every scientist felt that way. Even in her field she had experienced a sense of frustration because so many scientific advances made after she began her career could have been used to advantage had they taken place earlier.

At this time in his life Nelson had already received at

least twenty honorary degrees from various universities, was a trustee of important museums and educational institutions, and belonged to innumerable professional societies. Few of these honors meant as much to him as the accolade bestowed upon him in a speech by a man who had been his teacher and friend for many years. It occurred in October 1967. The College-Institute celebrated Nelson's twentieth anniversary as its president with a festive banquet at Cincinnati's Netherland Hilton Hotel, and the main speaker was Dr. William F. Albright.

In a speech entitled "A Hero of Biblical Archaeology," Dr. Albright paid high tribute to his former student. He praised Nelson for his most unusual persistence and intense application in learning the dating of Palestinian pottery. He traced the blazing trail his star pupil had begun during those early days in the American School which led to the recent establishment of the new Hebrew Union College Archaeological School and "its cooperative enterprise, shared by Jews and Christians, reconstructing the historical background of their common faith in Israel's God."

Pleased—and slightly embarrassed—Nelson listened as his teacher recited the milestones of his professional career. Was it really forty years since that fall day in Jerusalem when he had walked into Dr. Albright's lab for the first time?

Though he often wished for more time to pursue his work in archaeology, Nelson knew he wasn't yet ready for retirement from the College-Institute. In the fall semester of 1968 a new class of rabbinical students would stroll the green-bordered walks of the Cincinnati campus. Among them would be the first girl.

He liked Sally Priesand very much. He had sat in his study and listened to her when she had come from her home in Cleveland for her first interview with him. He

Dr. William F. Albright honoring his pupil, Nelson Glueck, on the 20th anniversary of Glueck's presidency of Hebrew Union College, celebrated at the Sherry-Netherland Hotel in Cincinnati.

Courtesy of Dr. Helen I. Glueck

Nelson Glueck's wife, Dr. Helen I. Glueck, and son, Dr. Charles J. Glueck, working together at the hematology laboratory at the University of Cincinnati Medical School.

Courtesy of Dr. Helen I. Glueck

Ancient pottery on display at the Nelson Glueck School of Biblical Archaeology, Jerusalem, Israel.

Courtesy of Dr. Helen I. Glueck

had been impressed by the brown-haired girl, whose eyes sparkled with intelligence and humor, and he had been affected by the determination she had to be the first woman rabbi in the history of modern Judaism.

It would be quite a struggle, even with her fellow students and her professors on campus. Nelson had encouraged her, for he saw in her qualities of strength and a fighting spirit. He also foresaw that her struggle would be in keeping with the traditions of American Reform.

Just as the main concern of the Reform movement had always been to adjust Judaism to the American environment, Nelson now felt it was right that a woman enter the exclusively male world of the clergy at a time when women were assuming roles of leadership in other fields also.

Nelson had always encouraged Helen to fulfill her talents in a medical career, and he had found that her success justified his steady support. He felt strongly that he should support the young girl from Cleveland who wanted to be a rabbi. Sally Priesand would need him this fall when she began her studies in Cincinnati. He wanted to be around to help her.

He had still another reason for wanting to remain in Cincinnati. He was a grandfather now. Remembering that he had been away so much during the childhood of his own son, Nelson hoped to spend more time with David, his grandson.

Both Nelson and Helen had been surprised when Charlie decided to marry so young. After all, both of the young people were only juniors in college, Charlie at Harvard, Barbara at Radcliffe.

"They're so young," Helen had exclaimed after Charlie brought Barbara to them and announced his plans.

Nelson, who was thirty-one when he got married, did not agree.

"You like her, don't you?" he had asked Helen.

"Oh, she's wonderful. It's just that they are so very young," Helen had replied.

"Well, that's all you can do . . . bring up your kids and hope for the best," Nelson had said.

Obviously Charlie did not consider himself too young.

In 1969 Nelson asked the Board of Governors to look for a successor for his post as president of the College-Institute. He wished to retire.

He was getting tired. He wanted time to sit and read, to publish his Negev findings, to teach his little grandson Hebrew.

He also felt it was time HUC-JIR had a younger man to lead it. The College-Institute had become four separate schools during his administration. Just traveling between them required stamina. The responsibilities, the decisions that had to be made almost constantly, demanded the energies of a younger person. After seventy even the most vital human being should no longer have to carry the burdens of such a responsible position.

The choice of a successor was difficult. It took the trustees over a year to make their selection. The Board of Governors chose Rabbi Alfred Gottschalk, head of the California School. As a "member of the family," Rabbi Gottschalk, who had been dean of the California School from its founding day, knew well the problems and challenges that lay ahead for the whole College-Institute. Nelson, pleased with the choice of Dr. Gottschalk, agreed to resign at the age of seventy-two, when he would become chancellor of the College-Institute.

Congratulations poured in from all over the world when, in 1970, Nelson reached the biblical three-score and ten years. A special *Festschrift*, written by twenty-three internationally prominent archaeologists, was dedicated to Nelson Glueck in honor of his seventieth birthday. Entitled *Near Eastern Archaeology in the Twentieth Century,* the book included essays contributed by colleagues and friends, men like Professor Albright, G. Ernest Wright, Pere Roland de Vaux, and Yigal Yadin, who had worked with Nelson and knew him well.

On October 23, 1970, the Feinstein Building was opened in Jerusalem on the campus of the Archaeological School. Its dedication also marked opening exercises for the first class of students in the College-Institute who would spend their freshman year in Israel.

The day dawned gray. In a land of too much sunshine, it never rained in October. That day it rained. The many friends and guests who had come for the opening, planned for the formally paved courtyard planted with slender saplings of olive, fig, and pomegranate trees, overflowed the chapel and packed the halls. They heard the guest of honor, Prime Minister Golda Meir, praise the Year-in-Israel Program as "an imaginative innovation to forge more strongly the links between Israel and American Jewry."

"Together with our own youth," said Mrs. Meir, "the students of the College will learn the great secret of our being one people wherever we may be."

"This is the happiest day of my life," Nelson said over and over as he and Helen greeted guests afterwards. No one who saw him that day failed to notice his happiness. His face alight with smiles, his full dark hair only barely sprinkled with gray, Nelson's whole being was radiating joy. He shook hands with close friends who had made the trip from the United States especially to honor him. He had words of congratulation for the students who made up the freshman class, many of whom had brought their wives with them to Israel. And, looking into their young eager faces, Nelson knew this was the day for which he had waited most of his life.

That winter, soon after their return from Israel, Helen suggested to Nelson that he see his physician. The doctor, while examining him, noticed a tiny growth in his neck which proved to be malignant.

Every day Mrs. Eleanor Vogel, Nelson's loyal archaeological secretary for many years, came to the house and worked with him. He dictated to her and spoke often of all the loose archaeological ends he wanted to tie up.

He had revised his opinion about the smelter at Eilat. Although he was certain he had found King Solomon's seaport, he no longer believed that the furnaces he had excavated there were used during Solomonic times and he wanted to publish these findings.

So many things were on his mind, so much was yet to be finished.

He wanted so much to see the Bar Mitzvah of his oldest grandson, David, but he knew now that he would not live for that day.

It was his great wish to ordain "Rabbi Sally" in the chapel of the Hebrew Union College. He felt strongly about being there when the first woman rabbi was to be ordained.

In March he and Helen would have celebrated their fortieth wedding anniversary, but as the first days of February approached, Nelson sensed he would not be there to share that milestone occasion with her.

"It's more like being married twenty years," he said to Helen, "we were apart so much of the time." He spoke often of his little apartment at the Jerusalem School where he kept his books, his typewriter, and his cameras, and where he had always hoped to return with Helen.

He longed to walk up that familiar incline on King

David Street in Jerusalem, to sniff once more the strong scent of jasmine in that garden half a world away. He wanted to stand on the terrace of his apartment from where, on a cloudless day, the mountains of Moab could be clearly seen . . .

But it was late. And Nelson knew it was time to go.

Epilogue

In the spring of 1973, exactly ten years after it was opened, the Hebrew Union College Biblical and Archaeological School in Jerusalem was renamed by the decision of its Board of Governors.

In honor of its guiding founder, it is today known as the *Nelson Glueck School of Biblical Archaeology.*

Bibliography

Albright, W. F. *The Archaeology of Palestine.* Baltimore: Penguin Books, 1960.
————. *The Biblical Period from Abraham to Ezra: An Historical Survey.* New York: Harper & Row, 1963.

Avi-Yonah, Michael, ed. *A History of the Holy Land.* Jerusalem: Jerusalem Publishing House, 1969.

Bentwich, Norman. *For Zion's Sake: A Biography of Judah L. Magnes.* Philadelphia: Jewish Publication Society, 1954.

Brilliant, Moshe. *Portrait of Israel.* New York: American Heritage Press, 1970.

Cottrell, Leonard. *Digs and Diggers: A Book of World Archaeology.* Cleveland and New York: World Publishing Co., 1964.

Deetz, James. *Invitation to Archaeology.* Garden City, N.Y.: Natural History Press, 1967.

DePaor, Liam. *Archaeology.* Baltimore: Penguin Books, 1967.

Glueck, Nelson. *Dateline: Jerusalem; A Diary by Nelson Glueck.* Cincinnati: Hebrew Union College Press, 1968.

————. *Rivers in the Desert: A History of the Negev.* Philadelphia: Jewish Publication Society, 1959.

————. *The Other Side of the Jordan.* New Haven: American Schools of Oriental Research, 1940.

————. *The River Jordan.* Philadelphia: Jewish Publication Society, 1946.

Keller, Werner. *The Bible as History.* New York: William Morrow, 1964.

152

Kenyon, Kathleen. *Archaeology in the Holy Land.* New York: Frederick A. Praeger, 1970.

Ludwig, Emil. *Schliemann: The Story of a Goldseeker.* Boston: Little, Brown, 1931.

Mann, Peggy. *Golda.* New York: Coward, McCann & Geoghegan, 1971.

Rapport, Samuel, and Helen Wright, eds. *Archaeology.* New York: Washington Square Press, 1969.

Rothkopf, Aaron. *Bernard Revel: Builder of American Jewish Orthodoxy.* Philadelphia: Jewish Publication Society, 1972.

Telling Tales out of School: Seminary Memories of the Hebrew Union College–Jewish Institute of Religion. Cincinnati: Alumni Association of the HUC-JIR, 1965.

Woolley, Sir Leonard. *Digging up the Past.* Baltimore: Penguin Books, 1972.

Wright, George Ernest, and Floyd Vivian Filson, eds. *The Westminster Historical Atlas to the Bible.* Philadelphia: Westminster Press, 1956.

Index

155